HOW TO STAND OUT ONLINE WITH CREATIVE CONTENT

JORDANA BORENSZTAJN

LONGUEVILLE
MEDIA

First published 2015 for Jordana Borensztajn by

Longueville Media Pty Ltd
PO Box 205 Haberfield NSW 2045 Australia
www.longmedia.com.au
info@longmedia.com.au
Tel. +61 2 9362 8441

Please note: The social media and online statistics that feature throughout this book were all accurate at the time of writing. By the time you read them, however, they will most likely have doubled, tripled or even quadrupled.

Front and back cover illustration and cover design: Bryan Webb (www.bryanwebbdesign.com). Under exclusive license in perpetuity to Jordana Borensztajn for Capture My Attention and other related works.

Credit for art elements used in the front and back cover illustrations:
Images: ©iStock.com/Carther and ©iStock.com/SilverV
Solid ink splatters: www.brusheezy.com/photoshoptutorials/Denny Tang

Copyright of illustrations on page 71 and 75: Ron Weed. Under exclusive license in perpetuity to Jordana Borensztajn for Capture My Attention and other related works.

ISBN (paperback): 978-0-9943862-0-5
ISBN (eBook): 978-0-9943862-1-2

National Library of Australia Cataloguing-in-Publication entry
Creator: Borensztajn, Jordana, author.
Title: Capture my attention : how to stand out online with creative content / Jordana Borensztajn.
ISBN: 9780994386205 (paperback)
Subjects: Online authorship--Handbooks, manuals, etc.
          Creative writing--Handbooks, manuals, etc.
          Electronic publishing--Handbooks, manuals, etc.
Dewey Number: 070.573

To my parents, Julie and Joey,
and my brother and sister, Noah and Sera,
thank you for always supporting
and encouraging my creativity.

ABOUT THE AUTHOR

Jordana Borensztajn is a creative content consultant, humourist and social media trainer who loves big ideas and new Apple products. She is a former News Corp Australia journalist, she worked as online music editor, content producer and social media manager at Nova Entertainment, she runs social media safety programs for schools, she speaks at corporate conferences around the world, and she's written and performed sold-out shows in the Melbourne International Comedy Festival. When Jordana's not busy helping clients develop and enhance their creativity, online content and social media marketing skills, you'll either find her taking selfies with miniature dogs or dressed as a giant Facebook Like button on the streets of New York.

Connect with her via:

- Twitter: www.twitter.com/jordanaoz
- Pinterest: www.pinterest.com/jordanaoz
- LinkedIn: www.linkedin.com/in/jordanaborensztajn
- Instagram: www.instagram.com/jordanaborensztajn
- YouTube: www.youtube.com/user/jordanaborensztajn
- Facebook: www.facebook.com/iamjordanaborensztajn
- Her websites: www.capturemyattention.com or www.jordanab.com
- A handwritten note sent by carrier pigeon

Contents

INTRODUCTION

The online world is noisy. Let's be honest: it's more than noisy. It's loud, it's chaotic, and it's so easy to get caught up in Facebook, Twitter, and Instagram that, before I know it, 15 minutes has turned into three hours and all I've managed to do successfully is watch YouTube clips with singing goats. You too?

Every hour, every minute, every second, millions of people around the world are posting, commenting, and chronically oversharing online. Our expectations of the content we consume are getting greater, while our attention spans are getting shorter. I don't even have the patience to sit through the first three seconds of YouTube advertisements. (The fact that you're still reading this far into the introduction actually says a lot about you – kudos.)

So, how can you make your brand stand out among all the chaos? You need creative content.

One of the most powerful marketing tools is differentiation, and the best way to have an impact is by being creative. In this book I'll share strategies, techniques, exercises, personal stories, and lessons from creative thought-leaders that will help you to think differently in order to get more creative and have a bigger impact with your brand online. Whether you're brainstorming video ideas for your next product launch, preparing images for an afternoon Facebook post, or developing a how-to guide for next week's blog, if you're willing to expand your perspective, step outside the norm, and get creative in your thinking, you'll gain a strong marketing edge.

With immediate access to endless information online, the more fun, unique, entertaining, relevant, thought provoking, and inspiring your content is, the more people will stop and take notice. You might only have one meme, one micro-video, or one well-lit and perfectly posed selfie to hold the attention of your audience. You can't assume they'll stay – quite the opposite actually, so being creative with your content is essential.

A lot of people, ironically, think of creativity in black and white terms: either you are creative or you aren't. I disagree. I believe creativity can be taught, inspired, and put into action, by everyone. There are strategies that we can all use, personally and professionally, to think more creatively when putting our brand – and ourselves – on show.

Creativity has pushed me to do things I once never thought were possible. I left full-time work to launch my own business, after years as a journalist, I became a stand-up comedian, and I travelled from Melbourne to Silicon Valley dressed as a giant Facebook Like. And I've created a lot of online content in the process.

I've written this book because each time I embarked on a new adventure, I Googled like crazy, trying to find tips, resources, and expert advice to make my road a little less bumpy. Learning from other people's insights and experiences has been of huge value to me, and now I want to give back by sharing with you the many lessons I have learnt along the way.

Capture My Attention is for anyone building their professional or personal brand online – marketers, business developers, small business owners, entrepreneurs, individuals, start-ups and more.

I show you how – with imagination, passion, character, and courage – to create captivating online content that will help you stand out, connect with your audience, and maybe even attract more attention than this week's most popular singing goat video.

Let's begin!

WHAT YOU SHOULD KNOW

Before we get into it

Before we get into the nitty-gritty, I want to take a brief moment to thank you for picking up my book. I'm honoured. The fact that you spent time in a bookstore and chose to read this is a compliment. Or maybe you bought it on Amazon or downloaded a free Kindle edition. Maybe it's not even your book and you borrowed it from your colleague's desk and they have no idea you nicked it. It doesn't really matter. All roads lead to the same place, and right now you're here with me. So, yay!

What's the best way to read this book?

Any way that suits you best. You see, I have a short attention span (I'm a digital baby, so it comes with the territory) and I struggle to read long books from start to finish, especially in one sitting. So I've structured each chapter to be self-contained, each with its own tips and/or exercises, to make it easier to read in short bursts. If you only want to read the chapters that appeal, go ahead. If you read it from start to finish, you'll see there's a logical flow, yet, it's designed to work whichever way you prefer.

I personally get the most value out of books that don't just speak to me, but also provide me with the skills and lessons needed to get started ASAP. I want to help you start creating awesome online content for your brand immediately, and I want you to be able to walk away with a long list of creative ideas when you've finished reading.

There are no time restrictions with the exercises. Do them quickly, do them slowly, start and come back – take whatever approach works best for your personal productivity and creativity. All I ask is that you take the punt and do them. Even if you start with just two minutes a day, every little bit helps. After all, if you do something new every single day, you're well on your way to forming a new creative habit.

Captures My Attention case studies

At *www.capturemyattention.com* you'll find links to all of the case studies, campaigns, videos, and images I refer to. Since there's nothing worse than clicking on dead links, I'll do my utmost to keep this list updated, so you never have to face the horror of a 404 error. A number of these may also be found in the reference and recommended media sections at the back of this book.

The big picture

Being creative with your content is just one small part of what you need to put together a killer content marketing strategy. There are many moving parts: content creation, identifying your content pillars, outlining your content goals, creating an editorial calendar, having the right team members in place, strategising your content sharing and social media tactics, outlining measurement methods for your content, and so much more. This book focuses specifically on content creation, because that's where my creative strategies are best applied.

You'll find more detailed information on social media marketing and content marketing resources in the list of helpful references I provide at the back of this book, and even more at *www.capturemyattention.com*.

Need more incentive?

This book is short. It's designed to be fun, including the glossary of terms at the end that reflects my individual twist on a variety of web words and social lingo. I hope to make you LOL while you learn. In addition to the tips, exercises, and stories, I've included jokes about selfies, Facebook, and BuzzFeed's quizzes – after all, it wouldn't be right without them.

If you're well versed in social media and you spend a lot of time online, enjoy, indulge, and tweet me your feedback at @JordanaOZ. If you're new to social media and online content, WELCOME! You're about to enter a world of status updates, Twitpics, and hashtags. It's time consuming and highly addictive. And, of course, lots of fun.

CONNECTING THROUGH CONTENT

Over the past decade, social networks have revolutionised the way we do business – in advertising, marketing, and customer service right through to fashion, political processes, and selfie-snapping CEOs.

Social media has completely transformed the way we connect with friends and family. I remember a time when we just didn't contact each other. Now, every day, Facebook gives me a list of people to say happy birthday to that I haven't seen since third grade. It's also changed the way we navigate and understand the world around us. Not long ago, everyone wanted to be a leader; now, everyone is happy to be a follower. These days it's better to join a trend online than set a trend in the real world, and the nerds are the powerful ones. Plus, now it's cooler than ever to study computer science in school. So many young kids dream of becoming the next Mark Zuckerberg.

Help! We have short attention spans!

The speed of social media, and the fact that we are constantly inundated with overwhelming amounts of information in our

Facebook News Feed, our fast-moving Twitter streams, and what feels like never-ending Pinterest boards, have all affected our ability to pay attention for any length of time. It's been really... uh, sorry, where was I?

We have 140-character restrictions in tweets, 15-second video limits on Instagram, and Vine only gives us six seconds to share our message. Six seconds! Our expectations of content are rising, while our attention spans are shrinking. We're learning to fit more into less, we don't want repetition, and we cut everything down with shortcuts, acronyms, and photos of our food. After all, they say so much more about us than we can ever put into words, right?

We hunger for awesome content

As everything in the online world continues to radically change, speed up, improve, and develop, one thing remains constant: our hunger for awesome content continues to grow.

We're sharing, communicating, feeling, responding, engaging, and interacting online now more than ever. We constantly want to be inspired, educated, and enlightened by great content. We are insatiable. We're consuming more content than we ever have and using far too many emoji in the process.

We are always on the lookout for videos, images, words, and online experiences that make us think, reflect, laugh, cry, or simply prompt us to cook something different for dinner (preferably shaped like a *Star Wars* character).

You have the tools to be awesome

The rise in user-friendly technology, software, and ground-breaking apps means we all have the ability to create more, with fewer skills than ever before, and, in many cases, just as well as the professionals (though don't tell them that). You can design a website with no coding skills, you can produce podcasts with zero audio editing training, and you can create your own memes and infographics without knowing anything about Photoshop. Anything is possible.

However, with all these easy-to-create programs, and even easier-to-publish options, comes chaos. The web is noisy, cluttered, and completely over-saturated. Creating content that will cut through isn't easy. Let's face it – we don't all own miserable-looking pets like Grumpy Cat and we can't all master epic drum routines like Justin Bieber at the age of 12. Unlike a filmmaker, whose audience is confined to a dark room for two hours with a giant screen and only popcorn to distract them, you're lucky if you get 15 seconds. And in most cases your viewer's 15 seconds is split via multitasking: while walking their dog, watching *Game of Thrones*, or pretending to tune in to one of their colleague's boardroom presentations.

'Marketing is a contest for people's attention.'

Author, speaker, and visionary marketer Seth Godin[1]

Get creative, get attention

You might only have one image, one infographic, or one Instagram video to hold the attention of your audience and get your message across. You can't assume they'll stay – quite the opposite, actually. So, being creative with your content is essential. Creativity requires an open mind, a playful spirit, and genuine passion. These are things we all possess, and they don't cost a dime. Creativity also requires time, energy, and commitment. And we are all capable of those too.

The best part – the beauty of creativity – is that no two ideas are ever the same. The way people navigate, explore, relate to, and express creativity is always different. If you invest time into brainstorming and fostering creative ideas in your workplace, within your team, and within yourself, they will pay off. Plus, you'll have a blast in the process.

'You can't use up creativity. The more you use, the more you have.'

Author, performer, and poet Maya Angelou[2]

Make your voice heard

In today's online world, we are all content creators. Do you write blog pieces? Do you create videos? Do you take iPhone pics? And do you share all of these across your social channels, on your website or in your newsletters? Then, yes, you are a content creator.

There has been a huge shift in power when it comes to the dissemination, communication, and sharing of information. In this modern, hyper-connected world, media companies no longer call the shots. Gone are the days when editors, chiefs of staff, and newsroom executives decide what is the most important news for us to consume. Sure, media companies source and publish countless online pieces, but it's everyone else who decides what matters. We decide what makes it to the top of the 'most read today' list. It's you, it's me, and it's all of our friends and contacts online who also Like, share, retweet, pin, and post the same content.

This dynamic provides us all with an amazing opportunity. For the first time in history, what you and I create can just as easily be shared across the internet, and circulated around the world, as content produced by *The New York Times* or *Entertainment Tonight*. (Yes, including that clip of you falling down the stairs at your prom. *Especially* that video.)

Individuals influence thousands, media companies are competing with stay-at-home bloggers, and fans and customers can directly impact the success or failure of a brand with a single *Yelp* or Amazon review. Now, more than ever, everyone around the world has the power to make their voice heard. So there's never been a better time to get creative and get noticed with your online content.

Relationships: Back to basics

In his book *Social Media Explained*, author, speaker, and university educator Mark Schaefer explains how the 'social' aspect of social media has changed the nature of marketing:

'The social web is simply bringing us back to our marketplace roots where personal connection, immediacy, and word of mouth validation are the most important marketing considerations. We're returning to the way people have ALWAYS wanted to buy from us – person to person. Humans buy from humans.'[3]

We all know relationships are, and always have been, fundamental to business success. Through online content you can personalise your brand in endless ways. Your visuals, videos, and, importantly, your written word serve as strong connectors to your audience.

Your content is your online self-expression

Your online content is one of your most important assets because it allows you to showcase your expertise in your field and boast your point of difference. It defines your brand, communicates your company message, helps you develop trust and loyalty with your audience, and, notably, creates a conversation point between you and your customers. And if it's done right, the content you share encourages engagement and triggers meaningful discussions that help humanise your brand online.

The value of this 'human' aspect is emphasised by digital thought-leader, futurist, and key analyst at Altimeter Group Brian Solis in his book *WTF [What's the Future] of Business?*, where he says that we live in an age where not only have brands become people but that people have become brands as well.[4]

And he's right. We have come to expect the same things from brands online that we expect from our friends. We want them to understand us, we want to connect with them, and on occasion we want them to pick us up from the airport.

You might have the best product in the world, but if information is hard to access online, if your website looks dated, if your buy links are clunky, if you ignore the questions I tweet to you and post on your Facebook wall and I feel like you're not listening to me, I'll dismiss you and move on to a competitor, without a second thought.

The power of killer content

Understanding the power that content can hold and using your insight and knowledge to create content that will help others will reap rewards. The best online content stirs a gut reaction, triggers emotion, promotes a call to action, and has the power to capture people's imagination sufficiently to momentarily transport them out of the world they live in and into the one that you create for them. If you create content with passion, purpose, and your customer's interests at the forefront of your content strategy, it will tell potential customers much more than just who you are and what you do. It will create a memorable and impactful experience that lasts far longer than a 400-word blog post or two-minute YouTube clip.

You may be thinking, 'Sounds great... but, um, how can I do all that with my content?' We'll talk more about how you can work these elements into your brand's content a little later.

Sayonara, old sales model

While many brands use social media to pitch and sell online, I'll tell you bluntly: it's damned annoying. Social media platforms aren't a place to blatantly pimp your product or flex your powers of persuasion. The whole point of social media is to be social, not sales-y. We're drawn to social media because it's a place where we voice our opinions, feel a sense of community, and share our family photos. So, when someone invades that comfortable space with a sales pitch, we feel like our privacy has been invaded. We don't want to be sold to online. It's that simple.

Content marketing matters

The rise in content marketing is proof that we're increasingly moving away from old sales models and embracing more integrated, engaged, and relationship-focused approaches. So, what is content marketing? Content marketing is more of a soft sell than a hard sell, basically. It's a marketing technique in which you create, share, and publish content with the intent to educate, entertain, enlighten, and help inform your customers. By positively impacting and improving your customers' lives with relevant information, you build trust, loyalty, and meaningful relationships, which turns into leads, and ultimately converts to sales.

Nobody describes content marketing better than the industry leader, the Content Marketing Institute:

'Content marketing is a strategic marketing approach focused on creating and distributing valuable, relevant, and consistent content to attract and retain a clearly defined audience – and, ultimately, to drive profitable customer action.'[5]

Every time huge brands like Coca-Cola and Nike unveil online content, each piece is a part of a much bigger content marketing strategy. What about you? What do you tell the world with your content? Are you trendy? Funny? Innovative? Are you a leader in your field? A socially minded company? Are you charitable? No matter what industry you work in, or what business you run, using content to communicate key messages and connect with customers is not just a savvy tactic; it's essential for businesses to move forward in today's online world.

Don't forget

- As the online world continues to grow, our appetite for engaging content grows as well. We are insatiable.

- Your online content is an important asset that allows you to personalise your brand in endless ways.

- You may only have one meme, one blog, or one Instagram video to hold your audience's attention and get your message across. Being creative with your content is essential.

- The best online content triggers emotion, drives discussion, and captures the imagination. It captures the essence of your brand.

MAKING A GOOD FIRST IMPRESSION

Whether we like it or not, first impressions count. In the real world we make judgements immediately, based on body language, hair colour, clothing, etc. I even judge people based on the model of smartphone they use. First impressions matter even more online because, in the absence of body language, eye contact, and facial expressions, all we really have to go on is the content we see in front of us.

Always remember: when you publish content, you're putting your brand on show for the world to see. (Or should I say the www.world?) Sometimes it's the very first exposure that people have to your product, idea, or service. So, it matters. From a lengthy blog post right down to an infographic, every single piece of content – no matter what it is – should be true to your core brand philosophy. Obviously, there are exceptions to the rule. For example, a six-second micro-video or a single image you post to Pinterest or Instagram cannot capture your entire brand backstory, but it should at least align with the overall vibe and sentiment of your product, or company message. It's helpful to always ask: *If this is the first piece of content somebody will see, does it capture the essence of what I'm/we're all about?* If your answer is no, it's time for a tweak.

Don't make these mistakes

When it comes to content, 'quality, not quantity' applies. Don't get me wrong, consistency matters, but quality should be a top priority. That doesn't mean you need to buy the latest and greatest digital camera to take high-quality Twitpics and YouTube videos – no, no, no. Quality means you need to offer real value to people who are giving you their time by watching, reading, or otherwise indulging in your content. And presentation counts. That means spelling, grammar, punctuation, audio quality, lighting, layout, and other elements need to be done right. Mistakes in content are unacceptable for brands showcasing themselves online. Here are a few reasons why.

Spelling mistakes in your title are equivalent to rocking up to a meeting with a massive coffee stain on your dishevelled, unbuttoned shirt. First impressions. It's the only thing people remember.

Creating **long-winded, boring content** that doesn't get to the point is like getting stuck with that guy at the party who talks about his badminton racquet technique. *Yawn.* Edit yourself. Edit, edit, edit.

Creating 'helpful' and 'expert' content that has **no constructive or useful tips** is like brewing and drinking a potful of decaf coffee. Correct me if I'm wrong, but what's the point?

Content that's too 'me, me, me' is every party anyone attends in Los Angeles. *No thanks.*

Carpe diem – or, rather, carpe content

Given how we move so quickly from window to window, and from tweet to tweet, if your video is too grainy, your audio too crackly, or your blog and article headlines are riddled with typos, if a potential customer clicks away, chances are they'll click away forever. Even if you attempt to lure them back later with better quality visuals or corrected spelling, they might never give you another shot – just like that second date that never happened. So, *carpe diem* – seize the day. Or should that be '*carpe* content'? Either way, put effort into making your content look good, because it really matters.

'Attention is a currency. We earn it. We spend it. Sometimes, we waste it.'

Author, speaker, and futurist Brian Solis[6]

Headlines: To click or not to click?

Headlines are important. The keywords you use, plus the style, structure, and overall punch of your headlines play a huge role in determining whether someone will click on your content or, instead, cruise right past it.

Keywords matter

Always include keywords and industry buzzwords in your headlines. What do people search for? What words would they Google when seeking answers to the questions your article or video addresses? *Include those keywords.* Not only do they help you show up in search engine results (referred to as SEO – search engine optimisation) but without them, nobody online will know that your restaurant serves the best mac 'n cheese in all of Wisconsin.

Three strategies for attractive headlines

1. Discussion points and questions. Ask questions as a way to stimulate intrigue and interest in your content. 'Could laughter improve your workplace efficiency and productivity?' 'Is your small business making these

three mistakes?' 'Can you eat five donuts in less than 35 seconds too?'

2. The classic journalism approach of including some of the 5 Ws: who, what, why, where, and when. If you make it clear to your audience, up front (or, actually, up top) what your content is all about, they'll know exactly what they're in for.

3. Make your headline about your audience by identifying how your content will help them. Be specific. People love numbers and lists and how-to pieces, and will click when adjectives are irresistible.

DON'Ts and DOs:

Don't do: Waking Up

Instead do: How to Wake Up on the Right Side of the Bed Every Morning

Don't do: My Latest Article about Coffee

Instead do: How Many Lattes Is Too Many Lattes?

Don't do: Losing Weight

Instead do: Three Tips to Lose Five Pounds While Chilling on the Couch

Make it immediately clear how your audience will benefit from consuming your content. Otherwise, why would they click on it when they could be watching that dancing giraffe video?

Tips to make a good first impression

- Spel chekk, spell chekk, oh, spell check. Confirm that all commas, semicolons, and capital letters are in the right place. Even spell check AutoCorrect fixes because they can slip past even the most efficient grammar geeks.

- Get to the point. Quickly, briefly, succinctly.

- Your headline is your hook, so lure readers in with juicy bait, including relevant keywords, industry buzzwords, and powerful adjectives.

- Make your customers the focus of your content. Instead of focusing on why your product or service is fantastic, focus on how your product or service can benefit and improve the lives of your customers. (More on this later.)

- Don't promote your content incorrectly. If you're offering tips, make sure they're valuable. If you're sharing news, ensure it's relevant to your audience, and if you tell people you're going to make them laugh, always have a spare cat-video compilation on standby in case your original content doesn't cut it: (click here for a cat video).

 Don't forget

- First impressions count online, and we judge brands based on the content in front of us.

- Put effort into making your content look good. If a potential customer clicks away, chances are they'll click away forever.

- Use your headline to draw readers in and make them aware of how your content will benefit them.

Chapter 3

THE PERFECT FIT: WHAT CONTENT WORKS BEST?

I know I've thrown around the phrases 'online content' and 'content creation' quite a bit. In the context of this book, they refer to anything that you create, compile, publish, post, and/or share with others – on your website, in your emails, and across your social media channels. This includes written words, audio recordings, images, video footage, animation and more. To give you some examples, here's a list of different content formats that you can pick and choose from, depending on what suits your audience and your business goals.

Content types:

- Blog posts
- News articles
- Photos
- Videos
- Micro-videos
- Memes
- Newsletters

- Infographics
- Podcasts
- Text, images, and video content for your social media channels
- Graphs
- How-to guides
- Lists
- PowerPoint and SlideShare presentations
- Repurposed content
- User-generated content
- Webinars
- Animated GIFs
- Cartoons and comics
- Company FAQs
- Any and all website copy

Feeling overwhelmed? Yeah, I felt overwhelmed just writing this list. Don't worry. I'm not recommending that you do all of them. Your priority is simply to create content that works for both you and your audience.

Trust me, I know what it's like to feel pressure to stay across the latest content trends and be all over social media. Most online marketers do. But don't give in to the pressure to launch a new social media account or a new short-form video series if you don't have sufficient time to build it and properly invest in it. You're better off focusing on just writing great articles, or compiling engaging newsletters, or creating fun text-and-image pictures for your brand's Instagram account. Then, once you've nailed that, work to expand your repertoire and your reach.

It's better to do what you do really, really well, than to be a jack of all trades and a master of none.

'I'm actually as proud of the things we haven't done as the things I have done. Innovation is saying no to 1000 things.'

Entrepreneur, tech pioneer, and Apple co-founder Steve Jobs[7]

What content is right for you?

Determining what content is right for your business is dependent on both your customers and you. Unfortunately there is no one-size-fits-all recipe, because that doesn't exist. The best way to find out what works for your brand is through trial and error. It's a fundamental part of the process, so, as you build your brand, make allowances for some content that hits and some that might miss the mark. This week a meme might work best, and next week an infographic might perform better. Be flexible and be open.

When deciding what content to create for your brand, remember that it's not all about you. A good understanding of your audience's interests and online habits is *paramount*, especially the way your product or service impacts your customers' lives. For a more detailed explanation, I've designed a walk-through exercise that I've posted online in case you'd like more help in answering these questions. Visit me at *www.capturemyattention.com* for a downloadable PDF.

Discover your team's hidden talents

When trying to work out what content to create, have a look within your team members' skill sets. Do you have any idea how many untapped skills your staff or co-workers possess that could be beneficial to the social media and online presence of your company? If you answered no, it's time to find out.

Ask your staff what they're passionate about, and what skills they have, above and beyond what's outlined in their position descriptions. For all you know, your receptionist might be spending three hours a night on Pinterest. That's an unbelievable amount of user knowledge you can access. Or you might have an assistant who is horrible at making coffee but has thousands of subscribers on YouTube. Now, I am not recommending that you assign the intern with no marketing skills to manage your social media strategy just because he loves Facebook. No way. However, your staff's online habits and extracurricular activities could be a valuable asset and source of insight when it comes to creating engaging and compelling content for your website and social accounts.

Exercise 3.1:

Uncover your staff's passions and interests

1. What are their hobbies?

Do they like knitting? Surfing? Are they big coffee drinkers? Great. However, none of those will actually help your bottom line. But if you have staff who spend hours of their own time blogging or making videos, they can help.

2. In the online space, where do they spend most of their time?

Facebook? LinkedIn? MySpace (what!)?

3. Do they have particular passions, skills, or interests that you don't know about, which they might be eager to share?

Are they teaching themselves how to edit videos in FinalCut or design posters in Photoshop? Or, do they spend weekends in a friend's basement laying beats and audio tracks?

4. Are there any areas of your business they would like to work on, contribute to, or add ideas, if given the opportunity?

Crafting Facebook posts? Writing blogs? Taking photos for Instagram?

5. What skills would they like to develop?

Understanding social media strategy? Analysing Google Analytics? Best and worst practices with Facebook advertising?

The sky's the limit

If you don't know the answers and can't cover these areas in regular discussions, consider inviting your employees individually into your office, and asking them: 'If you could do anything in our company in the online or social space, what would it be?' A former boss (thanks, Mike Cass) once asked me, 'If the sky was the limit, what would you want to do?' I can tell you it's an awesome feeling to be asked that. Of course, we can't all do what we want in a corporate environment, but when an employee knows that his or her skills, interests, and passions are valued, it can make a huge difference to their levels of enthusiasm and commitment.

Connecting the dots

Once you uncover where your staff's passions lie, and what skills they possess, match your employee strengths with your business's tech and content demands. You can start by letting them sit in on brainstorming sessions, or you can let them immerse themselves in their passion area entirely. The specifics are up to you. We know that people do the most productive work when they're passionate, so the idea is to create opportunities for your staff that allow them to direct their passion(s) towards your business goals. It will benefit both you and your employees ... or should I say your new designer, new photographer, new audio producer ... You catch my drift.

If you are a solo entrepreneur and want to develop some extra skill sets, start with whatever media, and medium interests you the most. You'll progress faster if you're enthusiastic about what you're working on.

Knowing what to avoid

It's also helpful to know what content you or your team *shouldn't* create, based on, well, a lack of skills. If there is a content format you want to create but you don't possess the right skills, don't worry. There are plenty of content alternatives. You *can* find the right fit without sacrificing quality. For example, if you're a bad speller, create a Top 10 list instead of writing a full blog piece, or if you're camera-shy, an audio-only webinar or podcast might be a better option.

 Don't forget

- Online content is anything that you create, compile, publish, post, and/or share with others – on your website, in your emails, and across your social media channels.

- Don't launch a new social media account if you're not prepared to invest time into building and developing it.

- Determining what content is right for your business depends on you and your customers. It's not 'one size fits all'.

- When creating content for your brand, it's not just about you. Understand your audience's interests and online habits, and how your product or service impacts their lives.

- Find ways to steer your staff's passions towards your business goals. We do our best work when we love what we do.

Chapter
4

GUT REACTION: WHAT MAKES CONTENT AWESOME?

Awesome content, just like an awesome photograph, has the power to move us, shape us and impact the way we see the world. It has the power to make us laugh, make us cry, and inspire us to take action. If it's really powerful, it can transport us into another world entirely, making us do the unthinkable online – stop multi-tasking, stop window-browsing, and stop refreshing our Facebook News Feeds. Oh, my.

But what makes great content? What are the common elements that hold our attention and draw us in? And can we identify and analyse characteristics that feature in popular content items, like Grumpy Cat memes, BuzzFeed articles, and Facebook posts by Boo the Pomeranian, that you can learn to incorporate into your own content strategy? The answer is yes. Definitely yes.

There are so many elements that contribute to killer online content: a captivating voice, strong visuals, engaging storytelling, and much more. While the exact ingredients for each brand vary depending on a company's creative vision and intentions, the end goal is always the same: to create a moving experience for your customers. You want to create content that will impact your audience's lives and provide value so they share it with their friends and followers, and ultimately spread your message for you.

To understand how to create impactful content for others, you must start by identifying the ways in which content impacts you. Let's start with your gut reaction.

Instinctive emotional responses

Google the words 'chimp adopts baby tiger' and what do you see? The cutest pictures ever, right? Did you break a little smile and feel warm inside without even thinking about it? Yeah, me too. That's because these adorable images triggered an immediate gut reaction, the way the best content always does.

The ideal content captures our hearts and our minds, and moves us the moment we first watch, read, or listen to it. Gut reactions are important because they're instinctive, and when we have an immediate emotional response to a piece of content, we're more likely to engage with it, and more likely to share it with our friends and followers so they, too, can experience the same feelings.

Now, neither you nor I have a crystal ball, and nobody I know can predict the future Nostradamus-style, so knowing exactly how an audience will react might strike you as all but impossible, but there *are* emotional triggers that we can identify and include in our content strategies in order to influence the experience our customers have when consuming and interacting with our words, videos, and images. Knowing what reaction you want to stir, and being clear about the message you wish to send, is important. But before you get there, you have to analyse how content makes YOU feel.

(Did you know, by the way, that your gut contains around 100 million neurons, which is more than what is found in your spinal cord?[8] So there is truth to the expression 'gut feeling'. Cool medical fact, right?)

So, what gut reactions do you have? Do you love a 'Top 10 Ways to Use Avocado' list? Do you hate a 'Pitch a Proper Tent' guide?

Are you constantly re-watching compilation videos showing Kim Kardashian bursting into tears on her reality show? If so, why? What exactly hooks you in or pushes you away? What emotions are stirred inside you?

I know they're not the easiest answers to articulate. That's the reason why so many people across the world pay hundreds, even thousands of dollars in psychologist and therapist fees – because so many of us struggle to get in touch with how we really feel. Trust me, I get it. But it's important because the way you make your customers feel is a key part of your brand experience and it should always be a priority in your content-planning process. The more you understand your own emotional responses to content, the better position you'll be in to incorporate triggers designed to generate emotional responses, into your content.

I have a few exercises to help you identify and articulate your own gut reactions, but let's first look at one of 2014's biggest celebrity social media news items: Ellen's group selfie at the Oscars.[9] It's a perfect example of a piece of content that prompted intense reactions across the world, and clocked up enormous statistics in the process.

Captures My Attention: Ellen's epic Oscars group selfie

In March 2014, Ellen DeGeneres broke Twitter (OK, not technically, but the social network did go into meltdown) when she snapped her now-famous group selfie. Photographed by *The Hangover's* Bradley Cooper, the photo featured Ellen alongside Angelina Jolie, Brad Pitt, Meryl Streep, Julia Roberts, Jennifer Lawrence, Kevin Spacey, Jared Leto, Channing Tatum, and Lupita Nyong'o and her brother. The epic Twitpic, which has since clocked up more than 3.3 million retweets, attracted so many eyeballs that Twitter temporarily crashed – right in the middle of the Academy Awards ceremony.[10]

When I first saw I this pic, I immediately gasped and laughed. I thought it looked hysterical, was amazed at how all these stars were happy to share the limelight, and it left me buzzing with questions: Are they all friends? Who arranged it? Was it staged? Did Angelina realise that half her mouth was cut out? Why is Lupita Nyong'o's brother in the photo? And did he take Liza Minnelli's spot?

The image was so powerful that everyone jumped on it and shared it: media outlets, bloggers – even people with dormant Twitter accounts felt inclined to log back in just to share this photo. I, along with millions of other people, had an immediate emotional reaction to it. It elicited all sorts of gut reactions: awe, amazement, intrigue, surprise, and more, not to mention all the people who just felt flat-out annoyed by it. Either way, millions of stories were created in response to, and around, this single image.

For the first time ever, the red-carpet dresses, award categories, and even the speeches at the Oscars were overshadowed by this single Twitpic. It stole the show, proving online content was the real winner of the 2014 Academy Awards. Yay, internet!

Captures My Attention: Dove's Real Beauty Sketch

Celebrities aside, heaps of brands create powerful online content that truly connects with audiences because it triggers a strong gut reaction. Dove's Real Beauty Sketch video is one example of branded content I will never forget. Dove's 'Campaign for Real Beauty' involves multiple clips, but I'm going to discuss the video that hit me the hardest.

In April 2013, Dove created a video titled 'Dove Real Beauty Sketches | You're more beautiful than you think' that spread an important message about self-confidence by focusing on the power of natural beauty, instead of beauty from a bottle.[11]

In this clip, a forensic sketch artist asks a series of women he cannot see to describe their appearance to him, and draws their sketches based on their descriptions. The artist then asks strangers who had briefly met these women a few hours earlier to describe their appearance to him, and draws a corresponding second set of sketches.

When the subjects view both versions of the sketches, we see the emotional moment when they become aware of the differences in the flaws they believe themselves to have, vs. the beauty others see in them. The clip ends with the message 'You are more beautiful than you think.'

This campaign exposed a universal truth about the harsh judgement we cast upon ourselves, and the imperfections so many of us perceive ourselves to have.[12] It was a wake-up call that highlighted the negative impact that self-doubt, body image issues, and a lack of self-confidence have on us all, insecurities the beauty industry has been using as a selling hook for centuries.

Their sketches, their expressions, their descriptions, the storytelling, the reveal, the message – all of these elements combined to hit a hard emotional core. It immediately made me stop and ask, 'What would I say? Would I do the same thing?' When I watched this video I felt guilty, self-conscious, ashamed, foolish, amazed, and in shock. It creates a major impact because it stirs a powerful gut reaction in its viewers, and, to this day, it continues to touch people, clocking up more than 66 million views and counting.

'But I don't have celebrity friends and I don't own a global skin product label! How can I publish content for my brand that makes people react?'

Well, it's easier than you think. Not all of us are A-list celebrities, but understanding and becoming hyper-aware of your own gut reactions is the best place to start. Knowing what makes you respond, react, ask questions, laugh, smile, feel inspired, be in awe, feel shock, or just feel sick to your stomach will give you a better idea of ways to incorporate triggers in your content that will encourage a gut reaction in others.

So, how does your favourite content make you feel?

Exercise 4.1:

Understanding your gut reaction

1. Go onto your Facebook profile and choose a piece of content you recently shared. Or, if you're not on Facebook, open up the last piece of content you forwarded to your friends in an email. Watch or read it again.

Yes, I'm serious. Do it now. Go on.

2. What feelings and reactions does it stir in you? List three of those emotions, and write down any words or phrases that come to mind.

Happy? Playful? Amazed? Maybe more serious emotions, like anxious, fearful, or irritated? If somebody was watching it with you, what would you say to them as soon as it ended?

'Oh, my God!' 'Are you kidding?' 'That's hilarious!' 'Awwww, so cute.'

3. What's different about this piece of content from others? What's unique or unusual?

The message? The point of view? The insight shared?

4. What are the strongest elements of this piece of content?

The images? The angle? The message?

5. Why did you choose to share it?

Will it make you look good/cool/smart/innovative/forward-thinking? Do you want your friends and family to also feel happy/aggravated/shocked/moved? Or perhaps you shared it to score bonus points from peers and/or colleagues?

Create a new habit: Identifying the value

From now on, every time you come across content that appeals to you, ask yourself questions 2, 3, 4, and 5. And keep a list of your answers. By identifying what content captures your attention, its strengths, and the emotions it stirs, you'll develop a solid understanding of exactly how and why such content adds value to your life. The more you understand about the way in which content impacts you, the more insight you'll have into how you can create content that will impact others. So pay attention.

OK, so that covers you and your reactions. It's equally important to understand the reactions of others around you. What do they like? What don't they like? And why?

Exercise 4.2:

Understanding others' gut reactions

1. Choose a piece of popular content that either you shared, a friend shared, or a brand shared across social media or in an email. Write down the content type, its theme, and its main message.

2. Did people engage with this content? If so, how? Likes? Shares? Comments?

3. Can you identify why they connected with it? What emotions/ reactions did this content item trigger in others (as evidenced by their comments)?

4. If you're on Facebook, now have a look at a piece that wasn't popular. Can you identify why people didn't engage with it?

Create a new habit: Identifying themes and patterns

Every time you post, create, and share content, write down what content items lead to engagement, and why. Also write down what content items lack engagement, and why. By compiling and building this list, you'll start to see patterns emerge which you can use as a guide to determine what content drives or deters engagement.

I hope this has provided you with some food for thought. Or emotions for thought. Or, if you're like me and you haven't gone through enough therapy to totally connect with your emotions, you can always check your emoji for inspiration. I can always count on tiny Japanese characters to help me express my deepest and most intimate feelings. Happy face? Sad face? A single red shoe?

When you understand how content makes you feel, and what feelings you can trigger in others, you're one step closer to understanding what makes people share, because emotions and sharing go hand in hand.

 ## Don't forget

- The best content captures our hearts and minds, triggering a gut reaction that leads us to share it – and your brand – with others.

- To understand how to create impactful content, you must first understand how content impacts you.

- The way you make your customers feel is a key part of your brand experience.

FEELING IT:
WHY DO WE SHARE?

There are many different theories and ideas on why we share content. I believe the fundamentals are pretty basic. Our gut reaction plays a huge role, of course, but ultimately it comes down to three core me-focused concepts. Sharing content across our social channels makes us look good, feel good, and helps us connect with others.

It's all about us

Sharing a TED Talk on protein biosynthesis makes us look smart and scientific; sharing a how-to guide on setting up a freshwater tank at home makes us look environmentally conscious; and sharing a charity link or petition against animal cruelty makes us come across as kind and socially aware.

Likewise, when we see a meme, image, video, or feature that makes us laugh, cry, smile, or feel warm and fuzzy, we feel great. And it's only natural that we would want our friends and followers to feel those emotions too, especially if we're the ones who show them. You have to admit that we each get a buzz from being the person who brings cool content to the attention of others. Especially if it's a new picture of Ryan Gosling without his shirt.

Plus, by sharing content we like, we reveal to our friends and followers what we're passionate about, what interests us, and what we care about. It's self-serving. And when they comment, Like, retweet, repost, and regram the same content, we see, in turn, what they're passionate about. Content is a powerful and often reciprocal online connector.

So, if you can create something touching, heartfelt, insightful, controversial, LOL-worthy or helpful – that will drive discussions *and* trigger a gut reaction – you'll seriously increase your share-worthy percentages.

Checklist: Is your content shareworthy?

1. Will your content impact a viewer's day in a memorable way? Will it provide value by teaching? Entertaining? Inspiring? Problem-solving?

2. Is it unique in its message/angle/ideas?

3. Does it look good, with eye-catching titles, punchy headlines, and relevant keywords?

4. Has it been edited down? Are you communicating in the simplest and most effective way possible?

5. Will it trigger a gut reaction? (That is, the kind you actually want?)

6. Will the person sharing it look good by posting it to their network? Will it make them look intelligent? Helpful? Good-humoured? Courteous? In-the-know?

Practise what you preach

Just making your content shareworthy isn't enough. You need to pimp it, promote it, and be proud of it. You need to give your audience the best chance possible to find it, learn from it, engage with it, and share it with their friends and followers.

At Content Marketing World Sydney 2015, I asked author, speaker, and social media influencer Jeff Bullas for the best piece of advice he could offer me specifically, based on his years of blogging success. He said (and he gave me permission to quote him here):

> **'Hustle your content. You're hustling in real life; you've gotta hustle online.'**

This really struck a chord. If we invest significant time and effort into creating content we believe will add value to people's lives, then we should spend just as much time proactively sharing it with the world.

 ## Don't forget

- Sharing content across social channels helps us connect with others in ways that make us look and feel good.

- When we share content, we share what inspires passion in us.

- Be proud of your content. Promote it. Give your audience the best chance of finding it, learning from it, indulging in it, and sharing it.

Chapter
6

CREATIVITY: THE CORE INGREDIENTS

What comes to mind when you think of creativity? Sculpture? Design? Poetry? Or maybe people, such as Steve Jobs, or Lady Gaga? If you ask a scientist about creativity, they'll likely serve up a left vs. right side of the brain explanation; if you ask a techie, they'll probably bang on about coding and functionality; and if you ask a comedian, they'll say 'my material!'

The way we each experience and relate to creativity is different. Creativity is far more than just an art form, an idea, or an expression. Those are important components, definitely, but not the entire picture. You see, creativity isn't just about a killer idea. Based on my experience, there are four key ingredients in the recipe for taking a creative idea and turning it into a reality:

1. Imagination
2. Passion
3. Character
4. Courage

Creativity is the product of all four of these ingredients. Imagination allows you to dream up your idea; passion helps you pursue your vision; character helps you define it, based on your insight, experience, and perspective; and courage helps you conquer your fears and follow it through – it's the willingness to take risks.

As someone who is driven by creativity, I can tell you first-hand that with creative thinking comes great freedom: the freedom to dream, the freedom to imagine, and the freedom to explore and express a side of yourself that you might not even be aware exists. Not only do we celebrate *being us* through creativity, but it's also a healing outlet; a way to externalise the internal and express the unexpressed. It can be liberating and therapeutic to bring to life, through creativity, what you would otherwise keep bottled up inside.

If you can encourage creativity, implement it, and use it to fuel and drive your content creation process, you'll rise above the chaos, because there is no greater tactic than a brilliant imagination.

'If you can dream it, you can do it.'

Cartoonist, animator, and producer Walt Disney[13]

Ingredient No. 1: Imagination

Imagination is where creativity begins. Our imagination allows us to dream up ideas, to see and envision new things. Driven by our thoughts and dreams, in this space anything is possible. Creativity can be one of the most amazing forms of self-expression, because our imagination knows no limits. If you truly open your mind, and indulge in your imagination, you can find a headspace that's free from the restrictions, judgements, and daily pressures that hold so many of us back. Not only is that type of time-out beneficial for our mental health, but the best part is that creativity inspires creativity. One idea leads to another, and another, until before you know it you're in a completely different spot from where you began, but it's a better place than you've ever been. (Unless, of course, you recently travelled to the Greek island of Santorini. That's a pretty mind-blowing destination.)

'I dream for a living.'

Director, screenwriter, and producer Steven Spielberg[14]

Ingredient No. 2: Passion

Creativity is fuelled by passion. No, I'm not talking about the *Fifty Shades of Grey* kind of passion. I'm talking about the burning desire and enthusiasm you feel when you love your idea and believe in your vision. We all face fear when working on creative projects, but if you can stay connected to your passion – the reason why you chose to do what you chose to do in the first place – it will act as a catalyst by providing the motivation you need to see your idea through. Plus, it will also inspire those around you, because true passion, and conviction, is contagious.

Passion invariably drives the career and life choices I have made throughout my life. I loved photography, so I launched my own business; I loved writing, so I became a journalist; I loved laughing (and wanted to avoid therapy fees), so I became a comedian; and I love being creative online, which is why I chose to write this book.

The best part is that passion makes it all worth it. If you believe in what you're doing, the journey and experience you embark upon will be worth undertaking, irrespective of the outcome. And what you'll find, in many cases, is that unexpected doors will open up along the way that may well be more beneficial and longer lasting than the original goal you had in mind.

'I just write what I wanted to write. I write what amuses me. It's totally for myself. I never in my wildest dreams expected this popularity.'

Harry Potter series author J.K. Rowling[15]

Ingredient No. 3: Character

Our character is what makes us 'us'. It's our individuality. It's our personal insight, experience, and perspective that we each bring to our creativity. I believe it is in our differences where our greatest creative strengths lie.

In an era when body image, bullying, and the amount of Likes, shares, and retweets significantly affect our self-esteem, creativity encourages and rewards our individuality, self-expression, and the value of real-world experiences. In fact, much of the negativity in the world is driven by discriminating against our differences: race, religion, sexual preference, etc. Conversely, creativity is enhanced by the very things that set us apart because our differences impact and enrich our creative output. All of the qualities that make us uniquely 'us' inform our creativity and contribute to our originality. This includes our backgrounds, opinions, beliefs, habits, friendships, and quirks. The way you drink your coffee, your favourite teen TV shows, how tidy you keep your kitchen, and even how you feel about Nickelback's songs influence your life and your perspective, the experiences you draw from, and ultimately, the ideas that you envision.

When I started doing stand-up comedy, I learnt pretty quickly that my differences were my greatest creative strengths. You see, in comedy, your worst attributes in life can become your greatest assets on stage. When you're honest and expose your vulnerabilities, you connect with people, but more importantly, it's your unique opinions, idiosyncrasies, and differences that make you memorable. So many of the world's wonderful artists are considered crazy because their work doesn't fit neatly within society's confines. But don't let other people's responses and reactions ever stop you. *Ever*. OK? After all, that's the whole point of creativity. The fact that your idea is different is why it stands out and has an impact.

Of course, we all want to fit in with our peers, colleagues, and friends, but at the same time, nobody wants to be ordinary. We can *all* be ordinary and that's just boring.

When I performed in my first comedy festival, I wrote an entire show based around my addiction to social media and technology. Instead of being embarrassed by my obsessive personality traits and habits, I drew attention to them, wrote jokes about them, got other people to laugh at them with me, and in the process created a distinct niche, and a memorable point of difference. It didn't get me any dates but it did fill the seats in my shows. And it was very, very therapeutic.

'Be yourself; everyone else is already taken.'

Writer, poet, and playwright Oscar Wilde[16]

Ingredient No. 4: Courage

Courage involves finding the strength to conquer our fears, even in the face of uncertainty. We need courage in creativity because it helps us turn ideas into action. It's the willingness to take risks, and it's what separates the people who *do* from those who merely *want to do*.

Do you have any clue how many incredible ideas that could have changed the world never saw the light of day because the people who dreamt them didn't even try to turn them into a reality? Well, I don't know the exact figure but I'm guessing it's millions. Zillions, even. So often, we might have this really cool idea that we're passionate about, but we find ourselves going 'No, I can't do this because my lawyer says no … or my friends say it's lame … or my sister tells me I'm "too old to become a professional pole dancer".' What truly sets apart the creatives you know from the creatives you don't is courage. Courage separates the dreamers from the DOers.

Now, I know courage isn't always easy to muster – we learnt that from the lion in *The Wizard of Oz* – but it's an admirable quality and one that will help you fight the fear you face. If you're passionate about your idea and confident it's worth pursuing, this alone will give you the courage needed to share your internal work with the external world. It's what moves you from *no* to *yes*, and *I can't* to *I am*.

I'm not suggesting you go bungee jumping, rock climbing, or hang gliding. I'm also not suggesting you leave your day job right now. Every creative decision needs proper thought, preparation, planning, and market research. What I am saying, however, is: Don't become one of the zillions. We have enough of them already. The 'you only live once' principle is something we should remind ourselves of constantly. It's easy to stick to a daily routine because it's comfortable, and it's tempting to stay in an unchallenging job because it's familiar. On the other hand, it can be completely nerve-racking to pursue a passion project – but, more often than not, it's so totally worth it.

'Some people want it to happen, some wish it would happen, others make it happen.'

Basketball star Michael Jordan[17]

A creative leap of faith

In 2008 I was a full-time journalist working at Melbourne's metro daily paper, the *Herald Sun*. It was a job that thousands of journalists would have jumped at, and I was thrilled to get it. I worked as an Editorial Assistant before getting accepted into the journalism cadetship program and I loved it: the buzz of the newsroom, the excitement of deadlines, and meeting and interviewing amazing people. But after what felt like a never-ending night shift, covering mostly doom-and-gloom police stories, I was burnt out and miserable. I was upset, unchallenged, and unmotivated, and I knew the role was negatively affecting me. The hours were affecting my social life, my energy levels, and my health. For months, I listed the pros and cons of the job, trying to weigh up being happy in the future, when I was 85 with a solid retirement fund, vs. being happy right then, at age 26. After much deliberation, the 26-year-old me won. I took a leap of faith and resigned from a highly sought-after position.

I was so unhappy with my career that I asked myself, 'What would bring me joy? Think big.' So I opened up my savings and bought a ticket to Africa to volunteer to work at lion parks, before heading to New York City to find work as a music journalist, which had become my new professional goal. It was scary, it was risky, and, like any creative pursuit, completely terrifying. The worst thing that happens when you embark on a creative endeavour, in my experience, is the fear of failure. I was worried I wouldn't find any work overseas and that I would have to return to Australia, feeling humiliated. Sometimes it feels easier to not try at all because that means you'll never fail.

My first stop was Africa. I spent two months volunteering at lion conservation parks, where I bottle-fed lion cubs, swam with elephants, and walked with 16-month-old lions (and I'd thought quitting my job was scary). Then I moved onto the second part of my dream: New York City. I arranged a work visa through a daily copywriting job and at night and on the weekends I was able to do my favourite things: I interviewed artists, reviewed gigs, and photographed bands at concerts and music festivals. Every day, when I walked out of my apartment at the corner of 7th Street and Avenue A in the East Village, I pinched myself at how lucky I was to be living in the best city in the world. It was a far cry from calling up Melbourne's emergency services in the middle of the night to ask, 'So, any muggings in the past hour?'

When you embark on a creative pursuit, trusting your internal compass is hard enough, but worrying about what other people will think can inflict 10 times the amount of pressure. Through this experience, I discovered something wonderful. I learnt that when you take a creative leap of faith, nobody actually judges you in the way you imagine. When I quit the newspaper, I received support from people in remarkable ways. The reality is that when people around you see you taking a risk, following your heart and having the courage to try something new, they respect you for following your dreams. Sometimes they're even inspired to find, and follow, their own.

Also, the reality of facing a situation in which you are unhappy, or desire things you don't have, can provide you with valuable insight into what it is you truly want. I waited till I hit my rock bottom at the newspaper before I became courageous, but you don't have to wait that long. Being courageous for you might not mean quitting your job and moving to Manhattan. It could mean enrolling in a photography class, learning to code, or starting that movie script you've dreamt about writing for years – whatever fires you up.

'You only live once, but if you do it right, once is enough.'

Performer and playwright Mae West[18]

Courage is about more than just an idea

Having courage doesn't just apply to what you do; it's also about being true to who you are, because that is what guides our passion. It's about having integrity and commitment. Consider Ellen DeGeneres. In a 2009 commencement speech delivered at New Orleans' Tulane University,[19] Ellen explained that after years as a successful stand-up comedian and having her own TV show to boot, she made the decision to disclose her sexuality to the world. She told the students of Tulane how she had been living with 'fear' and 'shame', and wanted to change her life. Her on-screen character, in *Ellen*, the TV series, had revealed the news the same time she had to the press. Despite her creative approach, she lost everything. Her show was cancelled and she didn't get any offers for three years. Yet, upon reflection, Ellen said she wouldn't do anything differently. In her speech, she explained how this experience helped her to discover the most valuable thing of all: the importance of being honest about who she is, what matters to her, and what she truly believes. Now, she pointed out, she lives a life without fear; a life in which she is free to be herself.

Today, Ellen hosts the most popular talk show on TV, she's responsible for the world's most popular selfie, and, as of July 2015, was sitting on a fortune of $75 million.[20] Clearly nothing beats honesty and integrity.

Creative icon: Lady Gaga

When it comes to creativity, no celebrity does it better than Lady Gaga. This ambitious, driven, New York City megastar has captured the world's attention for more than seven years. And she continues to capture it, over and over again. From her controversial red carpet meat dress to her powerful LGBT advocacy campaigns to her blink-and-you'll-miss them tights and underwear arrangements, Lady Gaga hooks us in. All the time.

I describe Lady Gaga as a creative icon because she embodies every aspect of my creative formula. Love her or hate her, she always grabs attention, she gets her message across in a captivating way, and she uses her individuality to stand out. Best of all, through her music, she encourages us all to embrace and celebrate our differences.

While her debut album *The Fame* spawned the unforgettable hits 'Just Dance', 'Poker Face' and 'Paparazzi', it was, in my opinion, Gaga's full-length, sophomore-delivery *Born This Way* that truly cemented her place in music history. This album changed the lives of millions of fans on a global scale, setting her apart from so many other musicians on the planet.

Why? Because, through *Born This Way*, Gaga offered far more than just killer hooks, catchy choruses, and sassy lyrics. The album's title track, 'Born This Way', captures a philosophy and spreads an important message that runs deeper than most No. 1 chart hits.

'Born This Way' celebrates our differences. The song promotes the belief that we should love ourselves the way we are, and rather than conform to the world around us, we should embrace our differences, because it's our unique quirks that make us beautiful. Through this powerful, empowering, and uniting song, Lady Gaga encourages us to be proud of the parts of ourselves that we have often secretly wished we could change.

We can all learn a lot from Lady Gaga's creative expression. Her extraordinary success shows us the unbelievable strength that comes from being proud of, and promoting, our individuality. Gaga is living proof that it's our differences that make us special and our uniqueness that makes us stand out.

'Don't you ever let a soul in the world tell you that you can't be exactly who you are.'

Singer and songwriter Lady Gaga[21]

Don't spend your life wondering, 'What if...?'

I want to share another story about courage. Consider it a 'backdoor route' to finding courage, if you will. Far worse than experiencing an enormous amount of fear is feeling huge amounts of regret. I learnt this lesson early in life.

When I was 14, I was obsessed with Julia Roberts. I watched *Pretty Woman* three times a week and knew every single word of the movie by heart. Tearjerker *Steel Magnolias* and fantasy flick *Hook* were also both on high rotation on my VHS player.

My parents decided to take us on an unforgettable family holiday to Los Angeles, where so many of my movie heroes resided, and I was so excited. As soon as I found out, I did my hair as big as I could to replicate Julia Roberts' best '90s do. Suffice to say, I was a massive Julia Roberts fan. She was my favourite actress and I simply adored her – even more than I did the Backstreet Boys.

A few days into the trip we were having lunch in Beverly Hills and about 10 minutes into the meal, I almost spat out my tuna nicoise salad when Julia Roberts strolled past. Her hair was up in a ponytail and she was wearing a baggy jumper and red leggings. She looked effortlessly stunning. I know people in America see celebrities all the time, but as a young, wide-eyed Australian teenager holidaying in the States, this was beyond anything I could comprehend. As it turned out, this was my first and last celebrity sighting in Los Angeles, despite many trips since.

With my excitement came sheer terror. I stood up from my chair and wanted to walk over to her. I wanted to tell her that I loved her movies. I wanted to ask for a photo. I wanted to bond over our curly red hair. But I couldn't. I was frozen. Crippled with fear and racked with nerves, my legs wouldn't move. I was overcome with doubts and insecurities: *I can't do this. She won't like me. She won't want to talk to me. What if I say the wrong thing? She's going to hate my Mickey Mouse t-shirt...* The list went on and on. Granted, I was probably right, and the last thing this film star would want was to be harassed by an Australian teenager with a waterproof Kodak camera and a desire to talk for hours about the nuances of Richard Gere.

In those few moments while I sat and listened to all of the reasons I gave myself *not* to approach Julia Roberts, my one and only chance of meeting my childhood idol was gone. I know that for some people this wouldn't be a big deal, but I have obsessive tendencies. Mix that with celebrity crushes and it's a lethal combination.

As soon as she was out of view, I sat down, shaking. I knew I'd missed my moment. Fear and adrenaline were quickly replaced with regret. Deep, soul-gnawing regret. I was devastated that I had let this opportunity pass simply because my nerves and doubts had gotten the better of me. This heavy feeling of not doing, not trying, and not knowing the answers to the 'what ifs' was overpowering. The only way I could cope with it was to make a promise to myself:

From this point on, if I'm ever afraid to meet someone, try something new, or do anything that makes me nervous, I'm just going to do it. I can't feel this way again.

And, over the past 19 years, I've stuck to this philosophy. And what I've discovered as a result is that the nerves don't last. Adrenaline and fear can feel completely overwhelming – and the courage needed to face your doubts and take a risk, when everything inside you is telling you otherwise, is incredibly challenging – but it's momentary, it's fleeting. Trust me.

Honestly, I could have lived with the awkwardness of me confessing, 'Julia, I love your hair and your big smile.' Even if she picked up her pace, kept her head down, or refused to take a photo with me, I could have dealt with that. Even a bad situation with Julia Roberts would be something that would make a good story later on. But it was the *not knowing* that ate me up. What if she would have really liked me? What if she'd commented on my great Disney shirt? What if we could have gone to her place to watch *The Goonies* together? I will never know.

To this day, when I see a Julia Roberts movie poster, or a Mickey Mouse t-shirt, the regret still gnaws at me like a dull ache. I never want to wonder 'What if…?' again. Life's too short. Consequently, this experience has been the driving force that's helped me take a lot of risks and conquer so many doubts over the years. Above all, it's taught me nerves are temporary but regret can last a lifetime. So, go on, take a risk.

It's all about you

When it comes to creativity, you don't need to paint with watercolour pastels, write poetry, or master life drawings to be considered creative. You also don't need to crack out of a giant egg on the Grammys red carpet to get noticed. Ultimately, creativity is all about you. It's about adding your individuality, your imagination, your passion, and your ideas into your online content, because that's what makes it stand out. Never underestimate what you're capable of. If you find the courage to bring yourself into your work, you've already made it unique.

'Have the courage to follow your heart and intuition. They somehow already know what you truly want to become.'

Entrepreneur, tech pioneer, and Apple co-founder Steve Jobs[22]

Don't forget

- The creative ingredients are imagination, passion, character, and courage.

- If you believe in what you're doing, your journey and experience will be worth undertaking, no matter the result.

- Our differences are our greatest creative strengths.

- Courage is conquering our fears in the face of uncertainty. It separates the dreamers from the DOers.

- When you follow your dreams, you inspire others to do the same.

- Nerves are temporary; regret can last a lifetime.

CAPTIVATE ME: VOICE AND VISUALS

Do you know what your brand's voice is? If I asked you to describe it to me in three words right now, could you? Is it irreverent? Is it serious? Or does it sound like a curly red-haired humourist from Australia? (If so, we would probably get along well.) If you can't describe it right away, don't worry. I know doing this can be difficult. Understanding what a brand voice is, and being able to define it, is not an easy task. However, mastering and executing a well-defined voice is fundamental to your online success, because your brand's voice is one of your most captivating online assets.

Your voice

Your voice isn't simply the words you write and the ideas you share with your audience. While those are important elements that help you communicate and connect with your customers, your brand's voice runs much deeper. It's so much more than just what you say to your audience: it's how you express your message and why you do it that way.[23]

Your voice is your attitude. It showcases your individuality. It helps you distinguish, and highlight, your point of difference[24] and it's what makes you stand out from all the other voices online.

Just as every character in a movie has a different voice, every brand, company and public figure has a different voice. And voice affects everything – the way you communicate your ideas, your word choices, your sentence structure, and your PUNCTUATION!! (See what I mean?) In the absence of body language and physical expressions on the web, your voice turns the experience of reading a blog piece, a tweet, or a newsletter into a personal one.

Just as your brand grows and develops, your voice can evolve. The way you define it now might be different to the way you define it in a year's time. The most important thing is to ensure that your voice is honest and authentic. It needs to reflect who you are and what your brand stands for.

And if you're working across multiple brands – a personal brand, a professional brand, and you moonlight as a dominatrix – you may need multiple voices. My voice as a comic differs from my voice as an author, which is completely different from my voice as a journalist. All of which are radically different from the voice inside my head constantly nagging me to lose another five kilograms.

Captures My Attention: Comedian Jenny Johnson

Sometimes voice can be so alluring that, irrespective of the context, you're hooked. Like comedian Jenny Johnson, for example. Despite the fact that I don't always agree with her political views, the risqué language she uses, or her harsh celebrity commentary, I regularly visit her Twitter account because I connect with Johnson's unique voice. Her comments on pop culture are delivered with such sharp and savvy wit, that I feel like I know her personally.

Here are three tweets[25] that offer a taste of Jenny Johnson's style:

> 'Can I have your gluten?'
> 'I have so much respect for people who eat inside Taco Bell instead of going through the drive-thru and eating in their car like garbage.'
> 'I'm happy Kim Kardashian is on another vacation in Mexico. She deserves to relax after all the hard work she's been doing.'

See what I mean? Johnson oozes personality. Her dry and sarcastic tweets are packed full of attitude. And her point of difference is clear: she makes fun of pop culture and popular trends. Johnson doesn't engage with her followers – she's not really one for interactions on Twitter – she mostly tweets to entertain. Her target demographic is anyone who is willing to laugh at themselves and the people around them, and that's definitely me. Plus another 413,000-plus Twitter followers[26] (and counting), so she's definitely doing something right.

Captures My Attention: Taco Bell

Another brand with a superb voice on social media is Taco Bell, in the States. While you wouldn't normally connect the words *smart* and *witty* with a Fresco chicken soft taco, the Mexican food chain's Twitter account[27] is definitely worth following. I'm not sure how long it took Taco Bell to nail its voice on Twitter – by the time I started following Taco Bell, it was incredibly well defined – but each tweet is like a tiny, humorous reminder that life might actually be a little better with a daily breakfast burrito.

Here are three tweets[28] that show exactly what I mean:

> 'Taco Bell gets me.'
> 'Taco Bell is my spirit animal.'
> 'I followed my heart, and it led me to Taco Bell.'

Or should that be: 'I followed my heart to Taco Bell, and it led me... straight to the cardiologist?' Either way, I'm in. Taco Bell has built a Tweputation (yes, that works) for being consistently entertaining. Not only does Taco Bell pack flair into its tweets, but it has a spiritual tongue-in-cheek vibe that gives off the impression that the next time you sit down to eat a spicy enchilada, it just might be an out-of-body experience.

In an impressive manner, the fast food giant creates social media posts that make its online experience a personal one. They respond to thousands of Twitter mentions, and even start conversations with people who simply reference their brand in their updates. Their online content communicates passion and a positive energy that makes it easy to connect with. And their voice is so compelling that their personality totally outweighs their product (which is great, because it's a far less fattening way to indulge in the brand). At a time when we are all cautious of how detrimental fast food is to our health, Taco Bell makes its Mexican menu items very desirable. *Hasta luego!*

Of course, not all brands are irreverent and quirky. Some are mature and informative, like CNN, some are aspirational and inspirational, like Nike, some are energetic and daring, like Red Bull, while others are bold and conservative, like Yves Saint Laurent.

Here's an exercise to help you crystallise and really focus on defining your voice. And if you don't know what your brand voice is, it's time to start creating it.

Exercise 7.1:

Finding your brand voice

1. What is your brand's core message?

What are your philosophies, values, and beliefs?

2. Describe your brand's personality in three words.

Are you adventurous? Honest? Intellectual? Down-to-earth?

3. Who is your target demographic?

How young or old are they? Where do they live? What are their interests? Visualise them. Imagine they're sitting in your office with you.

4. How does your target demographic like to interact?

What language do they use? Do they laugh? Are they serious? Is there industry lingo you should incorporate?

5. Think about your strengths and point of difference.

Why choose you over a competitor? What makes you stand out? What's different? What can you offer that the next guy can't?

6. Think about how you want to come across to your audience.

How would you speak to your audience if they were sitting right in front of you? Be conversational. Say it aloud before you write it online.

7. Using all of the information above, prepare some short, key messages for your audience focused on how your product or service will help them.

How will your product improve their lives? Save them money? Make them happier or healthier?

Style guide

Once you've made your way through the exercise points, put together a style guide outlining the language your brand uses online, including your voice characteristics, your key messages, your point of difference, special industry keywords and buzzwords, and writing DOs and DON'Ts, including rules for spelling, grammar, punctuation and more. Every time you make a mistake, add it to your DON'Ts list. Print out this style guide and refer to it as a refresher every time you create a new piece of content.

One brand, one voice

No matter how big or small your brand is, or how many staff are involved in creating your content, you need a single uniting voice across everything that you publish online. It's important that whoever contributes to your online content – you, your partner, your sales staff, your marketing team or even your CEO – understands your voice and stays consistent in its delivery. If that's not achievable, ensure that someone screens and monitors all posts and communications so that you stay on brand. Consistency is a vital ingredient when building online relationships.

Your visuals

No matter how stories have been captured and documented over the years – on carvings, on the backs of napkins, or even today through iMessage, one thing remains constant: visuals have, and always will be, one of the most powerful parts of the storytelling process.

As the old adage goes, 'A picture paints a thousand words.' This saying will always be relevant, especially in the digital world. In fact, visuals are one of the most powerful tools at your disposal. In this internet age of decreasing attention spans, we're always looking for shorter and more efficient ways to communicate. Visuals allow us to communicate messages and ideas in quick, innovative, and creative ways. Most of the time, sending a message, sharing a lesson, or bringing an idea to life visually has a bigger impact than just text alone.[29]

Why are visuals so powerful? Not just because the brain processes visual information much faster than text,[30] but because the experience of looking at visuals is exactly that: an experience. We have a gut reaction to visuals (and we know, from Chapter 4, how powerful gut reactions are). Visuals speak to our heart and soul, and capture a magic that can sometimes be impossible to communicate with words. This is why *Jurassic Park*, *Silence of the Lambs*, and *Forrest Gump* are just a few examples where the flicks gained way more momentum than their original paperback counterparts.[31] I don't know about you but I will never forget the scene where that Tyrannosaurus rex attacked the Jeep during a wild thunderstorm in Steven Spielberg's masterpiece. It's etched in my memory forever.

Statistical proof

The success of visually driven social networks like YouTube, Pinterest, Instagram, and Facebook is testament to the popularity of visuals. Just look at these mind-blowing social media statistics below to get an indication of their online picture proof:

- More than 350 million photos are uploaded every day to Facebook[32] (yes, mostly cakes and cookies)
- 70 million images are posted to Instagram every day[33] (yes, mostly selfies)
- 300 hours of footage are uploaded to YouTube every minute[34] (hopefully more goats singing Taylor Swift songs)

These stats are extraordinary. In fact, visuals have been the tools of success for many of today's biggest internet sensations. Justin Bieber attracted the attention of his future manager, Scooter Braun, with video footage from a local talent competition on YouTube, Michelle Phan rose to fame in the world of cosmetics with her YouTube make-up tutorials, and, K-Pop artist Psy became a household name when the world watched, shared, and tried to replicate his video, 'Gangnam Style'. Now look at him. He's... oh, wait, where is he now? Regardless, 'Gangnam Style' clocked up more than two billion views in two years, and, at the time of writing this book, held the record for YouTube's most-watched clip.[35] They're mind-blowing statistics.

Visuals pack punch

There are a lot of ways that visuals can help enrich, enhance, and strengthen your online content. I want to share three key approaches:

1. Show, don't tell
2. Think differently
3. Get emotional

Show, don't tell

Did you ever learn about the 'show, don't tell' philosophy? It's a literary technique I was taught in creative writing classes where a writer tells a story through a character's actions and speech rather than documenting every single feeling and thought they are having. Instead of outlining detail after detail, the goal is to set up a picture for the reader, but not give too much away. For example, if you tell the reader Tamara frantically paced around her apartment, muttering in broken sentences, with crumbs in her hair and still wearing last night's make-up, we get a pretty clear picture of her mental state. It's way more colourful and effective than just writing, 'When Tamara woke up, she was tired and on edge, and felt anxious and frustrated.' If you can find ways to show instead of tell, it'll be engaging, fun and in many cases, will have a deeper and longer-lasting impact.

'Show, don't tell' is entirely applicable to online content. For example, if you are promoting a weight-loss program, show me before-and-after images, instead of just listing weigh-in stats on your website. If your laundry detergent is the best on the market, show me footage of impossible stains it's removed so I'm left asking, 'How on earth did they do that?' Or, if you run a cosmetic clinic, I want to see a video testimonial from an 80-year-old woman who looks 45, thanks to brilliant Botox results, rather than simply reading about the strength of your service online. I imagine her piece to camera would be: 'This Botox is so effective, I'm totally wrinkle-free. Believe it or not, I'm actually smiling right now!' (See? It's more effective, right?)

Always ask yourself:

'How can I show what my product or service does, rather than tell it?'

Think differently

Use visuals to communicate your message in a way that people won't expect. Don't always go for the first image that pops into your mind. Think about related keywords and concepts and, excuse the cliché, but think outside the box. Don't be afraid to experiment because there is no perfect formula.

Get emotional

We react immediately to visuals, so always think about the message you want to send and the emotion you want to trigger. You *want* to strike an emotional chord with your visuals because, as I explained in Chapter 4, the way you make your customers feel is a key part of your brand experience.

It's really easy, at any stage, to get more visual. Here's a collection of quick techniques to inspire content ideas through your everyday office activity.

Quick ideas: Get more visual through everyday business activities

- When you present to clients and staff, is there a standard routine you always run through? Would it make a good how-to clip for YouTube?

- Do your colleagues make you laugh? Do they drop valuable nuggets of information in casual discussion? Get a notebook, write it all down, and search for photos that bring those comments to life. You've got yourself some fun new posts for Instagram or Twitter.

- Have a look back through your PowerPoint presentations and choose a few that have the most valuable industry or company insight. Post them on SlideShare.

- Are there certain questions your clients ask you repeatedly? What answers do you give? Can you turn these answers into short and succinct tips? If so, create an infographic, a meme, or a video. People love tips!

When voice and visuals combine

We've established that a brand's voice is an essential tool in online content. And we've also discussed the huge value and power of visuals. When you combine a distinct voice with compelling visuals, you can create a weapon of mass destruction – or mass virality, as is the case with Boo, the incredibly popular Pomeranian from San Francisco.

Captures My Attention: Boo the Pomeranian

If you type 'world's cutest dog' into Google, Boo dominates the search results. With more than 17 million Facebook fans,[36] two Boo books, a Boo calendar, Boo clothing, Boo mugs, and, yes, even Boo slippers, the tiny pup has captured the hearts (and wallets) of internet users all over the world.

No matter how many memes, videos, or articles fill my Facebook News Feed, when I see Boo content, I always stop what I'm doing to indulge in his posts. And, nine times out of 10, I share them. With adorable images and a positive life message, Boo's hard to resist. His Facebook 'About' page[37] perfectly sums up his sentiment: 'My name is Boo. I am a dog. Life is good.' I desperately want to adopt him as my own digital pet.

And he's right. Life *is* good for Boo. Boo has appeared on *Good Morning America*, his debut book *Boo: The Adventures of the Cutest Dog in the World* has been translated into multiple languages, and, during my last visit to New York City, I spotted a dedicated Boo stand in the world-famous FAO Schwarz toy store on Fifth Avenue. Boo's even been photographed with Liam Payne from One Direction. He was probably Liam's only fan who wasn't screaming when the pic was taken. Clearly he was trying to play it cool.

Of course, his insanely adorable photos make me melt inside, but aside from Boo's obvious and irresistible cute factor, it's his voice that makes my adoration for this little pup run so deep. The cheeky, positive, and innocent attitude that his owner gives him through the captions that accompany all of his photos on social media transforms his two-dimensional pictures into meaningful real-world experiences. The more I feel I know about Boo, the more I connect with him.

Here are three quotes[38] from his Facebook posts that illustrate what I mean:

> 'i sleep in the nude. wherever i want. whenever i want.'
> 'small dog, big world.'
> 'welcome to monday. how may i help you?'

It's undeniable that Boo's posts have an overwhelmingly feel-good effect. The captions that accompany Boo's photos are eternally positive and promote the things we all cherish most in life: love, friendship, and relaxation. The punctuation in Boo's posts – or, rather, the lack of punctuation – adds to the expression of his voice too. His sentences are short and sweet and there are no capital letters and no apostrophes. If you think about it, why would there be? He's a dog, and dogs don't do grammar. All of these tiny details add to the authenticity of his character. His owner has even used Boo's birthdays as an opportunity to raise and donate money to charity, which adds to his appeal (and helps counteract any negative feedback a little dog could attract from making squillions in merch).

Boo's irresistible charm and positive and playful personality make him distinctively different from any other cute cat or dog on the planet. You want to adopt him too now, right? Well, he's mine. *Mine!*

Captures My Attention: Humans of New York

Another online success story resulting from a powerful combination of voice and visuals is the amazing photo blog and Facebook page for *Humans of New York*. Created by photographer Brandon Stanton, *Humans of New York* is a collection of breathtaking portrait photos of the weird, wonderful, and beautiful people who inhabit New York City.

Brandon's original goal was to collect 10,000 profile pictures and chart them on a photo map of New York City. But, as the project progressed, it began to take on a life of its own, where the vignettes of the individuals he was photographing proved too engaging not to share. 'I started collecting quotes and short stories from the people I met, and began including these snippets alongside the photographs. Taken together, these portraits and captions became the subject of a vibrant blog.'[39]

Vibrant is a modest way to describe it. Today, *Humans of New York*'s Facebook page boasts more than 14 million fans[40] and his portraits get thousands of shares and comments. And it's no wonder

– his images are striking. But more than that, it's the way Brandon combines a subject's personal story with the expression captured in his pictures that really makes *Humans of New York* a truly unforgettable experience.

Alongside each image, Brandon features a quote from the subject that reveals something important about their life: their struggles, their hopes, their dreams. He shares their voice with us, and as a result we develop a deeper connection with them. It also makes us develop a more meaningful connection with Brandon. Not only do we appreciate his talent and artistry, but we admire him as a storyteller and narrator. Brandon chooses one special quote, thought, or idea from the subject to share with the online world. Because this quote fundamentally affects the way *Humans of New York's* fans and followers experience his images, we get insight into what moves Brandon on a personal level, and what parts of the human condition resonate with him the most.

Humans of New York is incredibly moving, and Brandon's images are stunning. I've included links to a few of my favourite *Humans of New York* pics at *www.capturemyattention.com*. Go on, take a few minutes (or hours) to check them out.

Start snapping

Don't let equipment restrictions limit your creativity. You don't need the newest and most expensive telephoto or wide-angle lenses to create killer online content. With HD cameras on all smartphones, and easy access to Vine, Vimeo, YouTube, and Instagram, we can all become modern-day photographers and videographers. Not to discredit media professionals who have trained and worked in these disciplines for years (I am a photographer so I've played on both sides of the fence) but the reality is that today's easy-to-use smartphone apps and desktop programs give us all the opportunity we need to create eye-catching visual work. Thanks to Instagram's filters, plus dozens of other cool photo and video-editing apps, each of us has the ability to combat lens flare, over-exposure, and of course, crop to perfection. We can all create visuals that will have an impact – no matter our background, skill set, or experience.

 ## Don't forget

- Your voice is more than just the words you write; it's how you express yourself and why you do it that way.

- Your business needs a single uniting voice across everything you publish online.

- Images boost the storytelling process.

- Visuals convey magic sometimes impossible to express with words alone. (Google 'cookies and cream'. See what I mean?)

- Visuals communicate messages in quick, engaging ways.

- Combine a distinct voice with compelling visuals to create something truly captivating.

- If equipment restrictions or a lack of real-world skills limit your creativity online, try the App Store.

HOOK ME IN: THE ART OF STORYTELLING

From *Cinderella* to *Snow White*, from *Great Expectations* to *Lord of the Rings*, stories have been around forever. Before we had books, movies, and BuzzFeed articles, our ancestors used fables, myths, legends, and folktales to pass down important traditions, values, and messages.

Whether captured on ancient parchments or in caveman carvings, or communicated through newspapers, novels, or 3D Hollywood blockbusters, stories have always been a fundamental thread in the fabric of society, because we all understand stories.[41]

No matter where you're from or what you believe, morals are universal. *Little Red Riding Hood* teaches us not to talk to strangers, *Beauty and the Beast* shows us we shouldn't judge a book by its cover, and we've learnt that money can't buy happiness from the Kardashians. We connect with stories, and the really good ones have a positive, lasting impact on our lives, staying with us long after the novel wraps up and the credits roll through.

Online storytelling is essential

In the online world, storytelling is essential. We all want to indulge in content that's genuinely worth the minutes it takes us to watch, read, or consume it, and storytelling helps add meaning to the messages you share in a truly memorable way. Plus, great storytelling adds emotion to a brand's content, which leads to better, and deeper, audience connections.[42] This is incredibly valuable when you consider how significant a role our emotions play in driving our social media activity. If customers love your product (or content), they'll tell you. If they like your story, they'll share it. If they don't, well, they'll make sure everyone knows that too.

We're drawn to social media because it's a place where we share passions, voice opinions, meet like-minded people, feel a sense of community, and come together to take action. We all have a voice online, and we all want to be heard. And conversations between brands and customers are more open, transparent, and public than ever before.

Storytelling helps brands connect, stand out, and, importantly, share their messages in fun, engaging, and inclusive ways.[43]

Storytelling is the experience you create

So, what exactly is storytelling online? People have different definitions, depending on their perspective. A copywriter's description will differ from that of a creative writer, who will tell you something equally different to a journalist.

To begin with, storytelling for brands online is a much broader concept than traditional storytelling. After all, we can't all write Shakespeare-style tweets or create Martin Scorsese-style YouTube clips. And, let's face it, it's going to be pretty tough to fit a protagonist, obstacles, and a story arc into a single Facebook post when promoting your latest range of toddler teething rings. While storytelling online can, and often does, feature powerful fiction-writing elements, when I talk about storytelling in online content, ultimately I'm talking about the experience you create for your customers. What are you showing your customers? How does it make them feel, and what impact does it have on their lives? Those are the key elements that guide my own experiences with brands I connect with, and content I gravitate towards online.

Brian Solis explains in his book *WTF [What's the Future] of Business?* that, to Generation C, the generation of 'connected consumers', experience is paramount. Brands, he says, need to actively construct the journey they want their audience to take. Why? Because that allows them to inspire and guide their audience down their intended path in order to have an impact on the connection consumers develop with their brand online.[44]

Similar to movies, novels, plays, and TV shows, the best stories teach us, provoke us, thrill us, entertain us, intrigue us, and make us want more. Whether you use visuals, text, or video, or a combination of all three, a story can capture an idea, an opinion, a product, a campaign, a message, or even a moment in time. While the path taken to create that 'experience' varies from business to business, and brand to brand, in my opinion, storytelling online falls into three categories: a brand's story, brand storytelling, and just telling a stand-alone story.

Brand story

In your brand story, you're the star. You're Marilyn Monroe. It's the tale of how your business came to be, the 'light bulb' moment of idea conception, how your business developed and blossomed, the tough moments, the major milestones, and the struggles you overcame in pursuit of your goals. Your brand story captures your philosophy, the essence of who you are, what you stand for, and your vision for the future.

The earliest version of Facebook was launched in a Harvard University dorm room in 2004. Originally created as a social network to connect college students, the social media giant now has more than 936 million daily users.[45] That's one hell of a brand story.

Brand storytelling

In brand storytelling, your customers are the stars.[46] By focusing on their journey, and how your product positively impacts their lives, you create a powerful, shared experience that you both celebrate.

Coca-Cola does brand storytelling superbly well by celebrating their product *through* celebrating their customers. Their About page on Facebook, as of September 2015, sums it up: 'The Coca-Cola Facebook Page is a collection of your stories showing how people from around the world have helped make Coke into what it is today.'[47] Basically, Coke makes its customers the stars of its brand, telling them that their personal Coca-Cola stories and experiences are important to the company because the customers are the driving force behind their global success. I don't even drink Coke but this positive and inclusive customer-centric focus makes me feel like a root canal would be a small price to pay for the thrill of being a part of this sparkling, sugar-filled global army.

Stand-alone stories

And then, of course, some brands create content items that are novel, stand-alone pieces. They might have a beginning, middle, and end, and leave you with important lessons. They might feature traditional elements used in classic storytelling, which can include story arcs, protagonists, goals, obstacles, problem-solving, and life-changing lessons. Or, maybe they employ humour tactics to make you laugh. Whatever storytelling approach you use, you can bring this form of storytelling to life in countless ways: through blogs and articles, micro-videos, images, LinkedIn Pulse posts, and even 140-character tweets. OK, you might need a series of tweets, but the point is that there are plenty of cool and creative ways to cover storytelling for your brand. And, really, anyone can create a story that gets people talking. You don't need a big budget. You just need a healthy imagination, time to brainstorm, a willingness to take risks, and a passion for whatever it is you're investing in creating.

Captures My Attention: Black Milk

One of my favourite brands in the online world is the innovative, savvy, and successful Brisbane-based nylon company Black Milk. Their online success is driven largely by their huge focus on storytelling. Let's start by looking at their engaging brand story on their website, penned by Black Milk CEO James Lillis.

Black Milk's brand story

'Our story starts a long time ago in a little yellow house, outside an unusually loud train station, surrounded by mango trees in Brisbane, Australia. I was broke and working odd jobs here and there in order to achieve my financial goals, which included such grand ambitions such as...paying rent. And buying noodles.'[48]

I don't know about you, but I pulled out my microwave popcorn as soon as I started reading this.

James goes on to describe how he pawned a CD player to buy his first sewing machine and reflects on the first item of clothing he ever sewed, how he spent every spare penny on stretchy fabrics, the first pair of leggings he sold, the rising popularity of his blog, the amazing ways in which his business grew and blossomed, and of course, the incredible support he's received from his online community throughout his wild journey.

Wrapping up, he says, 'Of course, some things will never change. I still love making clothes. I love seeing all the different ways girls style their Black Milk pieces. Yeah, I even still love eating mangoes. So who am I? Just the guy with the coolest job in the world. :)'

James's story is personal and down to earth. Learning about his humble beginnings, how he failed before he succeeded, how he grew his business from a one-man operation into a profitable global operation, and how he gets strength from his passionate team and adoring community, makes me immediately connect with him and his brand. Additionally, his friendly, witty, light-hearted tone is present through all of the company's email correspondence with customers. All of these personal touches help create a one-of-a-kind experience. Not only do I relate with James's journey, admire his passion, and adore his products, but by detailing his highs, lows, and other key moments in the Black Milk brand story – his story – he achieved what every brand dreams of doing: through the use of engaging storytelling I connected with him, and went from being 'just another customer' to someone who felt invested in James's vision and was rooting for his continued success.

Black Milk's brand storytelling

Black Milk's brand story isn't the only storytelling tactic the company has mastered. Black Milk also nails its brand storytelling – so well, in fact, that this Australian-born company now has legions of dedicated brand advocates around the world. How? Black Milk, in masterful fashion, makes every single part of the customer journey a memorable experience.

Think about the process when you typically purchase something online: *find, choose, pay, receive, the end*, right? Not with this fashion brand.

There's an exclusivity to being a Black Milk customer that only Black Milk customers understand. I love the way they create new and limited design runs so that every item feels special and unique. I love the way staff develop honest friendships with customers through banter on their social media accounts. I love the way they affectionately refer to their community members as Sharkies. But my favourite part is the letter you get when your package arrives. In James's signature sharp and amusing banter, he encourages his Sharkies to capture and share their own Black Milk stories.

James finishes the funny and warm thanks-for-being-a-customer-you're-the-best letter with a call to action: 'ps. As always, we'd love to see pics, so snap some selfies and post 'em up on the Black Milk Clothing Facebook page or on Instagram and hashtag #blackmilkclothing.'

You'll find hundreds of thousands of Instagram images with the hashtag #blackmilkclothing.[49] I can't even keep up with the amount of photos posted to Black Milk's Facebook page. By encouraging community members to take photos, and share them using a uniting hashtag, Black Milk puts the focus squarely on the customer, making them the brand's stars. But, wait – it gets better.

Black Milk reposts endless photos of customers wearing its products across its website and social accounts. And, trust me, everyone wants their Batman bodysuit bathroom selfie to be chosen for display. Black Milk makes it exciting for customers to become part of its online community and offers a brilliant incentive for customers to integrate its product into their lives.

In the process of rewarding customer loyalty, Black Milk creates powerful brand advocates by building a really strong sense of community among its fans and followers.

Usually when you make a sale, it's done. But not with this fashion brand. Black Milk has set up a cycle of endless love, driven by a unique customer experience. The story starts with Black Milk. Customers are then encouraged to create their own visual story with their newly purchased item. They share it with their friends and followers on social media and also send it to Black Milk, which goes on to share it with its entire community.

Through this approach, the clothing label creates a powerful, shared storytelling experience where their story becomes their customer's story, and their customer's story becomes their story. This incredible dynamic helps foster passionate brand advocates while ensuring their products live on well beyond the point of purchase. Black Milk's storytelling doesn't wrap up when the online transaction is complete. Instead, in many ways, it's just the beginning of the journey.

> *For more insight into Black Milk's storytelling approach, see my interview with Cameron Parker, former head of Black Milk's Sales and Marketing, in Chapter 13.*

Feeling the love with Black Milk

Art by Ron Weed

Captures My Attention: Tourism Australia

When it comes to brand advocacy, Tourism Australia does an exceptional job. It sounds boring, right? A government agency promoting tourism? Well, far from it. Tourism Australia has created a strong and dedicated online community fuelled by, and focused on, passionate members and advocates.

I watched Tourism Australia's Global Manager of Social and Content Jesse Desjardins present at both Content Marketing World Sydney 2014 and 2015, and I was blown away. There are so many things Tourism Australia has done right with its social media and content strategy, but I want to focus on one of the most striking tactics: its fan photos. Tourism Australia posts a huge variety of user-generated photos across its social media accounts.

One of my favourite ways to welcome in the weekend is with Tourism Australia's 'Friday Fan Photos' albums, submitted via their Facebook page[50] and app, highlighting beautiful images shot by people who live in, or have visited, Australia. When Tourism Australia posts the weekly collection of pictures, they give each photographer credit, tagging each image with the owner's name and/or website. Thousands – and I mean thousands – of people comment and share these stunning photos.

Just to give you an idea of the type of reach these photos have, I picked a random album posted last winter and it had 12,490 shares in its first six days online. Massive! The level of exposure this provides the shooters – both amateurs and professionals – is remarkable because it allows them to build direct relationships with other Tourism Australia followers, creating their own connections and building new business opportunities.

Tourism Australia has set up an incredible cycle where, by rewarding passion, they encourage passion. When Tourism Australia showcases an image, they're showcasing an individual's unique perspective, experience, and talent, while also showcasing how beautiful Australia is. This encourages excitement and positive feedback among those viewing and sharing the images, and fuels

Tourism Australia's active fans and followers to capture, and send in, their own photographs of Australia, which provides the organisation with even more user-generated content to choose from.

Everybody wins in Tourism Australia's set-up

It's pretty obvious that both Black Milk and Tourism Australia are excellent storytellers. In different, yet equally effective ways, they each create unique and unforgettable experiences for their fans, followers, and customers. Let's take a closer look at Tourism Australia's win-win model to see just how powerful their set-up is.

How Tourism Australia wins

- Tourism Australia gets cool points for inviting images from its community.
- The quality of images they choose to share sets the bar incredibly high for all of the photographers and amateurs submitting photos. You won't find any awkward family photos on this site.
- Their social channels are popular and fuelled by user-generated content; they are inundated with images to choose from.

How photographers win

- Amateur and professional photographers get access to giant new fan bases.
- Through sharing and showcasing their photos and passions, they create new connections with other like-minded snappers.
- Photographers get credit for all of the images that are chosen and shared, opening the door to new connections, leads, and business opportunities.

How Australia wins:

- Stunning images showcase Australia's beauty and make our country look amazing (sometimes more amazing than it really is).
- The breathtaking images lure in even more unsuspecting tourists.
- Through rewarding the passion of community members, Tourism Australia encourages and fosters a deeper investment in, and adoration of, Australia.

How the community wins:

- There's the thrill and delight of seeing beautiful photos all the time. Every single day. Don't believe me? Go and check them out. They're awesome!
- It's the perfect platform to connect with other passionate travellers for unique tips and travel insight.
- Community members are motivated to connect, get involved, and get active, thanks to the supportive environment.

So, who loses? Nobody

The albums have such brilliant photos that every time I see them, it makes me view Australia differently, like I'm looking through a tourist's eyes with rose-coloured glasses. Or maybe it's just the Instagram filter they used…

Feeling the love with Tourism Australia

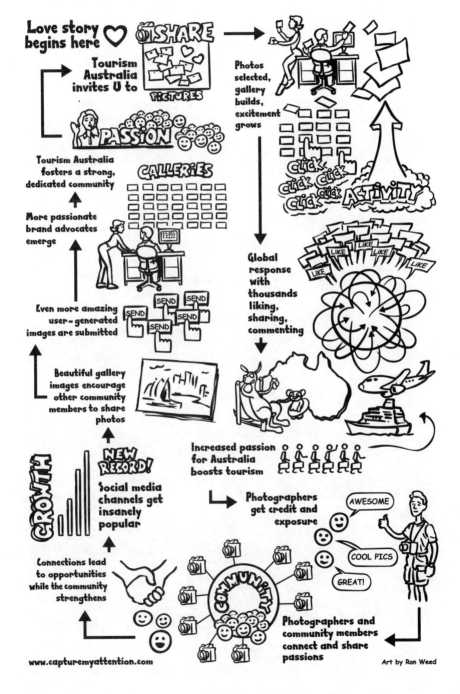

www.capturemyattention.com

Art by Ron Weed

You and your community

I know we don't all have the huge, adoring fan bases of Tourism Australia and Black Milk, but we do all have the opportunity to create powerful experiences online for our audiences. Depending on your product, service, and industry, there are a million different ways to create memorable moments with your fans, followers, and customers.

Below is a list of tips based on observations I have made of brands that have very engaged, passionate, and loyal online communities. Consider these points when thinking about ways to create your own unforgettable experiences with your community.

Tips to create engaged communities

- Invest time into building real relationships with your community members. At least give them as much attention as you do your daily barista.

- Listen to what your customers or followers say, seek, ask, and/ or need, and provide answers and insight.

- Encourage engagement by asking questions, retweeting, commenting, and sharing content. Just don't poke them. That's so 2008.

- Show constant appreciation. Your company, brand, and service is *what it is* because of your customers, so it's always a good time, and the right time, to thank your audience for their loyalty.

- Celebrate special moments and milestones with your community - not just Mother's Day and Christmas, but also reaching your first 100, 1000, 10,000 followers, and more.

- Be generous and forthcoming with praise. Don't be afraid to tell your customers why they're fabulous. We all love positive feedback. By the way, have I told you lately how skilled you are at reading this book? So talented…

- Create a strong sense of community. We all want to be part of something that matters, so create a sense of belonging and identity for your community members.

- Support and nurture your brand advocates. By rewarding their passion and loyalty, you'll encourage more advocates to emerge. If you play your cards right, they might even offer to pick up your dry cleaning.

- Give your fans, followers, and customers a reason to talk about you. Create a unique and emotional experience, providing value that other brands cannot match.

- Make your fans, followers, and customers look good. Promote them, highlight their wins, and share their best-looking selfies.

Any brand can reinvent itself with good storytelling

Now, I know you might be saying to yourself, 'I don't work with stretchy leggings, or fun travel photos. My brand storytelling isn't cool!' Any brand can influence the way it's perceived and reinvent its customer experience through innovative storytelling. Like Kmart, in the U.S., for example. They're far from a trendy brand. To be fair, they're unlikely to ever become a super-fashionable or ultra-hip retailer, though this reality didn't stop them from creating one of my all-time favourite branded content clips. Kmart released a 35-second video that was so unexpectedly playful, daring, and irreverent,[51] and so well received, that it went viral. More than 22 millions views and counting.

Some of you may remember Kmart's 'Ship My Pants' commercial,[52] where customers were offered free delivery on items they couldn't find in stores, through Kmart's 'Shop Your Way' rewards program. By combining a play on words with a little toilet humour and plenty of sass, Kmart showed customers that the brand has guts, flair, and a great sense of humour. In the ad, Kmart customers of all ages were saying, 'I just shipped my pants', as well as lines like, 'I just shipped my drawers', and 'I just shipped my nightie'. It's hilarious. No matter how highbrow we like to think we are, it appeals to the 12-year-old in us all.

What makes it even funnier is that it was created by a traditionally conservative company that, as far as I know, had never revealed anywhere near as much personality in any of its previous marketing approaches.[53] Would I consider using this ship-to-home offer? Maybe. Will I share this video across my social accounts because I think it's funny? Definitely. And in the process, I'll spread their message and contribute to the positive online buzz created from this ad campaign.

Be realistic: Assess the benefits and risks

You need a realistic and balanced understanding of the way your brand is perceived in the market – the good and the bad – to adequately assess the risks of your proposed content idea, and stack it up against the desired outcome. This Kmart ad was innovative and bold and different to anything they had previously done. On one hand, Kmart risked alienating a conservative customer base; yet, on the other hand, they stood to benefit by appealing to a new online-friendly demographic. Clearly, in this case, the benefits outweighed the risks. Because this video was unique and humorous, they attracted a lot of great press attention, which was testament to the video's success.

Promote the positive … and the negative

What people say about you won't always be kind, but don't assume a bad review, poor feedback, or negative chatter has to remain negative. Not at all. Naturally, you should review all feedback you get and respond appropriately, but also look for ways to get fun and creative. Like New York City's Joe & Misses Doe eatery, which turned a negative into a positive, in excellent fashion. I first saw this story on The Huffington Post[54] and absolutely loved it. This café copped a nasty Yelp review, slamming its meatball sandwiches. A fair amount of companies ignore bad reviews or try to defend themselves, but not these guys. Joe & Misses Doe turned this into a hilarious marketing tool. They placed a blackboard on the street, outside their store, that read: 'Come in and try the worst meatball sandwich that one guy on Yelp ever had in his life.' Gold, right? Even I'm tempted to taste one of their sandwiches now, just to prove this Yelp reviewer wrong – and I don't even like meatballs.

Listen up!

Good storytelling doesn't just involve publishing content and heading off to the pub. In order to tell a good story, you also need to be a good listener. You need to respond, participate, and engage. It's in your blog and emails, in your YouTube and Instagram comments, and in your Facebook threads and Twitter replies where you'll gain incredible insight into your customers' hearts, minds, hobbies, and complaints. Take the time to listen. You can discover what drives them, what motivates them, what they're passionate about, and what aggravates them. It's worth noting that these listening skills also come in handy when dealing with first dates, extended family … and women in general.

Also, don't view storytelling as a one-way process. To truly create powerful, shared experiences, they need to be exactly that: shared. So, find ways to work with your audience to create, develop, and grow your stories so they can be as hard-hitting and impactful as possible – for both your brand and your customers.

Your brand stories

Below are a variety of different brainstorming questions to consider, designed to help you navigate through your storytelling process. If you haven't started telling stories with your brand yet, it's never too late to start. Start now. And if you're already doing it, you can always get more creative.

Tips on sparking brand story ideas

When working on concepts and ideas for your brand story, ask yourself the following questions:

- How did your business begin? Where did the idea come from? What was the 'light bulb' moment when the idea first struck?

- Who was your first customer? Are they still your customer?

- What was your vision when you started? How has it changed?

- What was the toughest moment through your launch or growth?

- How have you celebrated your milestones?

- When did your business become profitable?

- Did you ever come close to quitting?

- What's your biggest achievement so far?

Your brand storytelling

The best brand storytelling captures and communicates the way in which your product impacts and improves your customers' lives.

You can invite your fans, followers, and customers to share their personal experiences with your product or service through text, photographs, video footage, or even artwork or other imagery. You can do this offline, online, or as part of a competition or prize giveaway. With their permission, you can then repurpose these text and visual responses and share them with your community in a variety of ways: features, galleries, video mash-ups, etc.

After all, what's more powerful: you talking about your brand, product, or service, or your customers talking about it for you?

Tips on prompts for brand storytelling

- How long have you used our product or service?

- What do you love about it?

- How is it different from others on the market?

- Why does it stand out?

- Why do you keep buying/using it?

- How does it make your life easier/better?

- Have you done anything incredible with it?

- Do you use it with your friends?

- Do you use it in funny/unexpected ways?

- Have you had any WOW moments with it?

Your stand-alone stories

A stand-alone story can be a six-second video on Vine, a blog entry, an experience you create for your audience through a Facebook post, or even a 12-month video campaign. It can be a single piece of content, or a single concept made up of multiple content items. These stories can directly focus on your product and customers or they can be unrelated, and designed purely to provide some entertainment. You can create a story that links to a popular news item (more on that in Chapter 10) or you can pick and choose a few compelling fiction-writing tactics to include in your storytelling to add extra depth and impact. Always think about the emotion and sentiment you're conveying to ensure you choose the right story format that your customers will connect with.

Storytelling inspiration: Fictional building blocks

Want more story ideas? When it comes to including traditional storytelling elements into online content, even Hans Christian Andersen would struggle to squeeze them all into a one-minute YouTube clip. But you can definitely feature the best one or two for added impact.

Goal. What's the story's overall purpose/mission/aim?

Protagonist. Who's involved? Why is this character or person here? What is it, specifically, about them?

Challenge. How can this character achieve their goal? What series of events needs to take place?

Obstacles. What stands in this character's way of achieving his/her goal? What risks do they face? What could interfere with their mission?

Change. What extraordinary experience do they go through in their journey? What has been tested, challenged or changed through this process?

Lessons. What do they learn about themselves through this journey? What do they learn about the world around them?

Takeaways. How can the rest of us learn from their lessons and their experiences? And how can we apply it to our own lives?

Story arc. Is there a chronological narrative? Is there a beginning, middle, and end? How does the storyline play out?

Climax. Is there a peak point? A major drama? A moment of high intensity?

 ## Don't forget

- A story online can capture an idea, an opinion, a product, a campaign, a message, or a moment in time. Ultimately it's about the experience you create for your customers.

- Storytelling online falls into three categories: a brand's story (where you're the star), brand storytelling (where your customers are the stars), or telling a novel story.

- To create powerful, shared experiences with your audience, they need to be exactly that: shared. Make your customers a part of your brand's stories.

- With innovative storytelling, even a company that manufactures manila folders could become cool. It hasn't happened yet, but it could.

Chapter
9

ENTERTAIN ME: ADD HUMOUR TO YOUR TOOLKIT

Before I started writing my own stand-up comedy, I was in awe of comedians: their sharp wit, their brilliant observations, and especially the way they put a new spin on the everyday, mundane scenarios we all experience. I would watch them, admiring them and asking myself, 'How, how, how do they do that?' As I studied humour, I discovered that beneath all great comedy material, strong comedic principles can be found. Sure, we can't all riff like Joan Rivers and Robin Williams, but there are formulas, theories, and equations being used by the best in the business that you can adopt and adapt into your own content to add a little sparkle.

We can all learn to be funny

That's right. You read that correctly. We can actually learn to be funny – funny is something that can be taught. Many people mistakenly believe we need to be born funny in order to be funny, which means either we have a great sense of humour or we don't. While a large part of our sense of humour is definitely instinctive, like many other creative and writing disciplines, comedy is an art form. And within it, you can find rules, structures, and formulas for comedy theory that can be uncovered, taught, and put into practice by everyone: comedians, Hollywood screenwriters, you, me – and, yes, even Herman from the mailroom.

While comedy can (and does) serve as a wonderful outlet to express many deep and dark truths, I don't want to be responsible for digging up, and unleashing, your personal demons so I'm not going to focus on soul-searching stand-up comedy here. I'll leave that to the professional comedy coaches who have the skills and experience to give you the help (and therapy) that you need. After all, I'm still learning so much about comedy myself. Rather, I want to focus on sharing the humour principles, theories, and strategies I have picked up, developed, and implemented over the past four years – strategies I put into practice every single day.

If you have a solid understanding of joke structure, joke ingredients, and different types of humour, you'll possess the necessary skills and knowledge to identify where, and how, to add the right amount of humour into your content to make it stand out.

How do I know this? Because I taught myself to be funny. Just a heads up – this next paragraph is going to sound very 'me, me, me', but soon we'll get to how it can be all about you, you, you. OK? OK.

My stand-up comedy journey

My comedy journey began in 2011, when a blind date went horribly, horribly wrong. It was an absolute disaster and left me feeling mortified, alone, and drained of all of my positive energy. When I told the story to my friends, recounting, line by drawn-out line, what he had said and what I'd said, they found it hysterical. They were laughing so hard at my misery that I started laughing too, and by the end we were all in tears of laughter. That laughter changed everything. It turned the whole situation around, making me forget just how shocked and upset I had felt a few hours earlier. It was a powerful revelation and in that moment I realised: *Comedy is so much faster and cheaper than therapy. I need to do this because it's therapeutic.* So I made it my mission to become a comedian.

In August 2011, I cracked open my first comedy book, *The Comedy Bible,* by Judy Carter, and there was no turning back. I read countless other comedy books, listened to as many comedy audiobooks as I could get my hands on, and made a commitment to write every single day. I joined a local comedy group for beginners, started doing open-mic nights, took part in a local comedy course, and worked with Judy over Skype. She was my first comedy coach and opened my eyes to so many things in comedy, especially the importance of attitude and act-outs, when structuring my jokes. Two months later, I did my first five-minute stand-up spot in a Melbourne club. Since then, I have performed at clubs in Los Angeles and New York, and have written, produced, and performed two sold-out shows in the Melbourne International Comedy Festival, plus a season in the Melbourne Fringe Festival. I also perform corporate comedy, and when I deliver keynotes and training presentations, I always use humour to deliver my most important messages. I have had an absolute blast over the past four years and can't imagine life without humour.

My comedy journey is proof that we can all learn to be funny – or anything else we want to be – if we're willing to put in the work. And consume lots of caffeine and chocolate in the process.

The rules and principles of humour are accessible to us all, and applicable to content creation; blogs, how-to guides, video scripts, social media updates, memes, and more. So, now, I want to take this opportunity to share the lessons I have learnt, and the processes I have in place, because seeing the world through a comedian's filter has changed the way I view everything – for the better. I draw from these principles each and every day, professionally and personally.

Why humour?

Humour is a powerful business tool, allowing us to create an instant connection. That connection can be to a person, an idea, a concept, or an experience. No matter who you are or where you're from, we all love to laugh. It's universal. Laughter improves our health and helps alleviate stress, plus it boosts our immune system by releasing endorphins, which are physiologically proven to make us feel good. Even if someone has never heard of your brand and doesn't use your product, if you make them laugh with a video or image online, they'll connect with you. Why? Because when we genuinely laugh, we're engaged and 'in the moment' which, for businesses in today's age of digital distraction, is an epic achievement.

'Making someone laugh is the most intimate connection you can create in a business context... without getting a call from HR.'

Comedy writer, MC, and Cisco Senior Marketing Manager Tim Washer[55]

How much humour?

Let's just get one thing clear: unless you're a comedian, you don't need to be funny all the time. Nobody will expect that from a brand. However, if you can find ways to make your online content a little quirkier, and packed with a little more LOL-worthy attitude, it's a powerful tool that can go a long way in helping you stand out. So, when I talk about adding humour to your content, I'm not talking about creating the kind of content that makes people roll around on the floor. Unless you've got Jerry Seinfeld, Larry David, and Ricky Gervais sitting in on your content strategy meetings, that's unrealistic. It's more about creating content that momentarily takes people away from where they are and gives them a warm, positive, and happy feeling. Just taking them out of their world for a brief moment can have real impact, because even a small dose of humour can have huge benefits. Whether it triggers a smile, a giggle, or even a chuckle, humour can make your content unforgettable. It gives your content a distinct point of difference and makes your brand stand out in a massive way. And it can be simple to accomplish.

What makes us laugh?

First and foremost – and you undoubtedly know this already – comedy is subjective. What makes you laugh can be entirely different to what makes me laugh. As comedy is an art form, the way we each express humour, and respond to humour, is different. So you'll never win everyone over with the same piece of content. But don't let that stop you. By all means, try.

The first step in understanding how to craft something funny is to understand what funny actually means. Why do we laugh? What makes something hilarious? There are multiple ingredients involved in writing a good joke: setup, punch line, etc. But on the most basic level, I find there are two fundamental elements that make or break every good joke:

1. an element of surprise;* and
2. the attitude you convey**

In order to illustrate these fundamentals, I'm going to use stand-up comedy examples. You don't have to be a stand-up comedian to write funny content, but when you look at all of the comedy genres – whether it be sketch, improv, slapstick, etc. – stand-up comedy writing features the tightest joke structure. I believe that if you

---

* I first learnt about the value of a joke's surprise element from Greg Dean's book, *Step by Step to Stand-Up Comedy*.

** I first came across the importance of attitude in jokes from Judy Carter's book, *The Comedy Bible*.

understand joke structure basics, you'll be in a better position to understand how to apply humour strategies into your online content.

The element of surprise

Jokes that generate the biggest impact reveal something unexpected, something that surprises us, a turn that we didn't see coming. It's when we're led down a path and all of a sudden the direction changes. This turn can be a truth, a moment, a thought, or a discovery. This turn creates a gap between what we *think* is happening and what is *actually* happening. And it's in this moment of revelation that we laugh. Sometimes we laugh at what this revelation says about us, and sometimes we laugh at what this truth exposes about others, but in all cases we laugh because we're confronted by a visual, a thought, or an idea that we didn't anticipate, expect, or envisage. Some comedy coaches refer to this as 'shattering the assumption'.

Here are a few one-liners that illustrate my point perfectly.

Ellen DeGeneres:
'My grandmother started walking five miles a day when she was sixty. She's ninety-seven now, and we don't know where the heck she is.'[56]

Zach Galifianakis:
'I have a lot of growing up to do. I realised that the other day inside my fort.'[57]

Groucho Marx:
'I never forget a face, but in your case I'd be glad to make an exception.'[58]

In all three jokes, the comedians take us in one direction before swiftly hitting us with a punch line that we don't foresee, conjuring up a funny image in the process. Did you picture Zach Galifianakis inside a fort made entirely of ferns? Yeah, me too.

Your attitude

The partner element to the element of surprise in any joke is your attitude about what you're expressing. Are you angry? Stressed? Frustrated? Confused? Irritated? Your attitude is the way you think and feel about the observation, gripe, joy, or grievance you're sharing. Your attitude can change from joke to joke, but one thing must remain constant: you need emotional motivation behind why you're saying what you're saying. It's a comedian's individual point of view on a specific topic that gives meaning to the opinion they're expressing. And when it's driven by true emotion, it has an impact. And, in most cases, the stronger the attitude, the funnier the joke.

Different types of humour

Behind every laugh triggered by a video or meme is a comedic strategy. In order to know how to apply humour to your content, it's important to understand as much as possible about the different types of genres within humour:

- observational
- sarcasm
- deadpan
- self-deprecation
- parody
- irony
- satire
- puns
- slapstick
- blue

When I started in comedy, I was familiar with the concepts of sarcasm, satire, and parody, but it wasn't until I studied them as methods that I really understood how to apply these principles to my writing. You might be familiar with these comedic genres and you might not. Even though not all of the genres are applicable, or suitable, to online content, I have found that developing a thorough understanding of different comedic styles and approaches has proven very helpful to my comedy writing. So I'm going to cover them, because the deeper and richer your understanding of all forms of comedic approaches, the more strategies and ideas you'll have to draw from when creating your own humorous content.

Observational humour

Observational humour is often the comedy of choice for some of the best in the business, like Jerry Seinfeld, Louis CK, Richard Pryor, and Robin Williams. It's where you find a new meaning, interpretation, intention, and/or explanation for the everyday stuff that we all experience. Observational humour is often intelligently written and has the power to challenge our views, make us see things differently, and impact the way we live our lives. Or, it can be as simple as laughing at a different perspective we've never previously considered. I love observational humour.

> Like this gem from Jerry Seinfeld:
> 'The road less travelled is less travelled for a reason.'[59]

Sarcasm

You're being sarcastic when you use a positive attitude in a negative way. In most cases, the comment is witty, like that of Bill Murray, who always delivers hilarious sarcastic humour. Ever watched *House*? Dr Gregory House, played by Hugh Laurie, is bitingly sarcastic. Did you watch *Friends*? Chandler Bing, played by Matthew Perry, was sarcastic in the best way possible. Or, if none of those references resonate, just ask any teenager if they're excited when their mum asks them to do their homework, wash the dishes, or take out the trash. I can guarantee they'll have a sarcastic comeback up their sleeve.

Deadpan

Delivering a joke or idea with almost no emotion, as a means of eliciting a tonne of emotion, is deadpan delivery. It's dry. It's where emphasis and enthusiasm for the story you're telling is replaced with a distinct lack thereof. The humour comes from the contrast between the meaning of the idea or opinion, and the lack of expression in its physical delivery. Like comedian Steven Wright. Every joke he delivers is expressed in the same, flat, monotone manner. A word of caution about deadpan humour, however: it's very dependent on facial expression, tone, and performance. Deadpan humour in online content can work when it's accompanied by visuals; it can too easily get lost in text-only content items.

Grumpy Cat[60] perfectly demonstrates deadpan humour communicated through visuals. Grumpy Cat, the famous cat from Arizona, whose real name is Tardar Sauce, suffers from feline dwarfism and also has an under-bite. This combination gives her a permanently grumpy expression. The internet is littered with hundreds of memes that are hilarious because of the deadpan humour that comes from combining messages with attitude, through the text, alongside Grumpy Cat's 'miserable' image.

Here are three examples of text that feature on popular Grumpy Cat memes:[61]

'I purred once. It was awful.'
'The worst thing after waking up? Everything until I go to bed again.'
'Greatest meme of 2012...whatever.'

Self-deprecation

Don't want to make fun of other people? That's a good instinct. It can be more fun – and far safer – to poke fun at yourself. The best benefit of self-deprecating humour is that nobody will likely get mad or offended when you are your biggest target (on the surface, anyway). Self-deprecation works really well for comics; however, I would recommend caution before denigrating your brand or product. Much like the Joe & Misses Doe example in the previous chapter, you want the public to be laughing alongside you, not at you. What they were really poking fun at was the review posted on *Yelp*, not their own product. When in doubt, it's better to avoid doing this, in case it backfires.

Parody

Parodying is using a celebrity, persona, popular subject, or well-known content item as a basis for ridicule. Weird Al Yankovic is one of the kings of parody. He uses hooks and rhythms of popular chart hits to draw us in, before putting his own spin on them.[62] For example, Michael Jackson's 'Beat It' inspired 'Eat It', Queen's 'Another One Bites the Dust' inspired 'Another One Rides the Bus'. And Robin Thicke's 'Blurred Lines' inspired one of his best parodies to date – and 3:46 minutes of heaven if you're a grammar and punctuation nerd like me – 'Word Crimes'. Likewise, *Scary Movie* was a parody of the successful *Scream* movie empire, and Leslie Nielsen's classic *Naked Gun* series was a spoof of pretty much every cop show on TV at the time.

Irony

Irony occurs when something you didn't expect, happens. It can be an action, event, attitude, or opinion that directly contrasts with what you would imagine or anticipate. Ironically, I had difficulty coming up with an amusing example of irony, so here's a real one: a swimming teacher who drowns. That would be devastatingly ironic. Not funny, of course, but definitely ironic.

Satire

Satire is parody with underlying social commentary. It's where you use humour to make a point, communicate an opinion, or directly comment on societal and social issues that affect us all as a means of drawing attention to whatever it is you're making fun of. The subject of satire can be an individual, a group of people, an organisation, or even a mindset that people hold.

> Nobody does it better than Sarah Silverman:
> 'People are always introducing me as "Sarah Silverman, Jewish comedian". I hate that! I wish people would see me for who I really am – I'm white!'[63]

In the world of animation, *South Park* is a top example of satire. Creators Matt Stone and Trey Parker make fun of pop stars, religion, news, current affairs, politics, and societal taboos. Absolutely nothing is off the table for Cartman, Kenny, Kyle, and Stan, in their small-time Colorado town.

Puns

A pun is a play on words, playing up a double meaning (often referred to as a *double entendre*). Despite making many of us groan, puns are getting more and more popular. Puns traditionally take a standard statement and make us rethink it. Remember this one? *Police were summoned to a daycare centre because a three-year-old was resisting a rest.* Think 'dad jokes'. Recently, puns have come to include creating words that sound alike or look alike – like saying 'they're punny' instead of 'they're funny'. Well, did you laugh? Some puns are super-basic, some are really lame, and some can be genuinely hysterical. Choose yours wisely.

Slapstick

Slapstick humour is physical, absurd, over the top, and completely exaggerated. Think Charlie Chaplin or the Marx Brothers and you've got it. It's where the humour is served up for you on a silver platter and it's so obvious that it hits you in the face. In fact, you couldn't miss it if you tried. It's every clip you've ever watched on *Funniest Home Videos* where people trip, slip, collapse, or fall over backwards.

Blue humour

Gutter humour, or blue comedy, whatever you want to call it, often involves crassness, swearing, and/or overt sexual references, and offends plenty of people. Yes, it usually gets laughs, but they're cheap laughs because of the shock factor. I would not recommend employing this type of humour when promoting brand content, unless you can find a way in which to weave it in, in a subtle way. Unfortunately, most of the time blue humour is used, it's classless.

Tips on using humour

- Identify and understand your brand voice and attitude *before* you try to be funny with it.

- Don't push a funny joke, meme, or video if it's not in line with your brand's values and vision.

- Know your audience and show respect for them.

- Remember that humour is subjective; people can be easily offended.

- Assess the risks on a case-by-case basis.

- Don't tell jokes that are offensive, sexist, racist, vulgar, or down-right rude.

- Don't mock other people or brands - it just makes you look bad.

Humour strategies

The rule of three

Three's a crowd in life, but in the comedy world, three's a charm. It's a magical number that lends itself to laughs. Why? We all understand the pattern of three; it's been embedded in our lives for centuries. *Three Little Pigs. Ready, set, go. Lights, camera, action.* A list of three provides a brilliant opportunity for a joke because of the pattern set by items one and two. When you replace the third item with something unexpected – a turn – that surprise becomes funny. It's the unanticipated change in direction between where we think we're heading and where we actually end up that makes us laugh.

When you're writing down a list, or working with a collection of bullet points, try to turn your points into a list of three to get a laugh. Alternatively, if you mention two similar ideas in the same sentence, turn that into a list of three by making the third idea something unexpected.

You can do this in sentence form:

- My New Year's goals are to get fit, get healthy, and get better at hiding my chocolate collection.
- I'm not picky about my dates. I just want them to be kind, thoughtful, and featured on the BRW Rich List.

- When taking photographs for Instagram, I carefully consider composition, lighting, and which filter will best address my insecurities and desperate need for attention.

Alternatively, you can do this in list form:

Top 3 tips for small business owners

1. Prepare a plan.
2. Prepare your finances.
3. Prepare to not sleep. At all.

Or, you can feature a surprise turn at the end of a longer list.

Your editorial calendar should outline your:

- Content goals
- Content topics
- Target audience
- Social media tactics
- Caffeine and tequila breaks

Try incorporating a list of three or a surprise turn in your next blog, how-to guide, or grocery list. See what I did there? Go on, it's fun!

Exaggeration

Another fun comedy tactic is exaggeration. Exaggeration is making something so far-fetched, so ridiculous, and so outrageous that it becomes funny. It's a great tactic to use when creating content, as it allows you to spread an important message about your brand, business, or product in a fun and original way. How? Start by identifying the answers to the following three questions:

1. What's the objective of your product or service?

2. What is the most extreme situation you could solve with your product or service?
3. How can you use this 'worst-case scenario' to trigger a call to action and convey your message?

Let's say, for example, that you're a chiropractor and you want to remind patients to come in for regular checks.

Q: **What's the objective of your product or service?**
A: To improve people's posture.
Q: **What is the most extreme situation you could solve with product or service?**
A: Bad knees, bad neck, or a bad back.
Q: **How can you use this extreme scenario to trigger a call to action and get your message across?**
A: Imagine an image of a hunchback of Notre Dame-type character who'd represent a major challenge for any chiropractor, right? He's in his castle, in a dark and gloomy corner, hunched over his brand new smartphone, tweeting. Your caption reads: 'Don't wait until it's too late. Get your spine assessed today.'

If you're not into cartoons, but you still want to remind patients to come in for regular checks, how about this:

Text-and-pic overlay

Picture: A teenager is hunched over his smartphone.
Text: 'When's the last time you had your spine checked?'

Or, let's say you manufacture kitchen products and you want to promote your new super-heat-resistant oven mitts. How does this video script sound?

Video

Scene 1: Kitchen, indoors. Husband takes food out of the oven and burns his hands. In pain, he dashes to the sink and runs his hands under cold water.

Wife barks at husband, waving oven mitts in his face: 'How many times have I told you? Use oven mitts!'

Husband: 'OK, OK, you're right! I'll use them!'

Wife: 'Promise?'

Husband: 'I promise!'

Scene 2: Backyard, outside. A two-metre-long strip of burning coals is set up in the backyard. Husband, wearing oven mitts on his feet, is walking across the coals. His best friend stands alongside the coals, chanting: 'Go, go, go!'

Scene 3: Shot of kitchen window, from outside. Wife peers out the window. Her eyes widen in shock. She starts banging on the window, yelling.

Voiceover: 'Our oven mitts can withstand the heat. Can you?'

Common knowledge as comedy inspiration

Drawing on commonalities – things we all know about and share in common – is a great source for humour. Using clichés, idioms, stereotypes, and assumptions provides a great basis for jokes because they provide a set-up and expectation that needs little, if any, explanation. The key here is knowing how to use these common elements to your advantage.

Using clichés

Clichés are phrases and expressions that at some point in the past were innovative, universally apt, and sometimes poignant; however, after excessive overuse, have lost all of their charm. Instead of being meaningful, they've become annoying, repetitive, and tiresome due to years of overexposure. That said, they're an excellent source for brainstorming material. Why? Because the very fact that they're ubiquitous means we all recognise clichés. If you can put an original and funny spin on a tired cliché, reinventing it and giving it new meaning, it can be quite refreshing. Plus, because of our familiarity with clichés, they create visuals that we can all work with. We can either build on this idea or shatter the assumption entirely.

Here are some clichés that would likely make your eyes roll.

1. An apple a day keeps the doctor away.
2. All's fair in love and war.
3. Love is blind.

If I was creating content for an Apple reseller, *Game of Thrones*, and an optometry clinic, respectively, here's what I would go with.

Text-and-pic overlay

Apple reseller

Picture: Apple logo
Text: 'An apple a day keeps tech support at bay.'

Text-and-pic overlay

Game of Thrones

Picture: Graphic montage from *Games of Thrones'* new season
Text: 'All's fair in *Game of Thrones*.'

Video

Optometry clinic

Frame 1: Silhouette of young couple in love.

Frame 2: Text added to the image, which reads 'Love is blind.'

Frame 3: Footage of the silhouette reforming to show it's not a young couple – it's actually two seagulls.

Frame 4: Image of the seagulls reduces in size as the text reads: 'But you don't have to be. When's the last time you had your eyes tested? Come in for a free consultation.'

Clichés can be a rich source of inspiration for visuals you create and share across your social channels. As annoying as they might be, don't dismiss them. Keep your eye on the prize. (See what I mean?)

Using stereotypes

Stereotypes are generalisations: thoughts and judgements that we make about living creatures, most often groups of people. These judgements are typically based on race, gender, demographics, geography, anyone working in a particular industry, etc. Most stereotypes are myths, with no factual basis. They survive and are passed down from generation to generation through sheer ignorance. Yay for humans!

In comedy, breaking stereotypes can be really fun. Here are a few classic examples:

1. Blondes are dumb
2. Women are bad drivers
3. Accountants are boring
4. Politicians are liars (OK, maybe this one isn't a myth.)

You can use stereotypes to your advantage by shattering their meaning, or exaggerating them enormously, which can be extremely funny. Let's look at one common stereotype as an example.

If I owned a party hire company, I would create a video that shows a pumping nightclub party, with drinks, lasers, and a DJ. And it's packed. I would show still shots on a time lapse: 9 p.m., 11 p.m., 1 a.m., 4 a.m., where each party frame has fewer and fewer people. By 4 a.m., there are just five men left on the dance floor. Their ties are off, their shirts are flapping open, and they're partying hard. Pop-up text reveals their name badges and the firm at which they work.

Voiceover says: 'We can even keep accountants up late. Contact us to host your next party.'

I want to share a word of caution, however, regarding stereotypes. If you make a joke with a stereotype at its core, like a joke about women being bad drivers, you run the risk of offending half your audience (maybe more, since we women outnumber men these days), and coming across as myopic and narrow-minded. A much safer and more fun way to use stereotypes is by taking them to the extreme and busting them entirely. That way you're not supporting the naïve view of the stereotype; instead, the subject of the stereotype actually wins, like the hard-partying accountants in the example above.

More tips on using humour

- **Google a list of clichés.** Can you put a funny spin on any of the classics in a way that relates to your brand?

- **Look up a list of stereotypes.** Are there any that relate to your industry or customers? Are there any myths or generalisations you can break down?

- **Exaggerate, exaggerate, exaggerate.** Go the extreme. If your product can do A, B, and C, can you imagine if it also did X, Y, and Z? And what would that look like? If your customers love white-chocolate-covered raspberries, how far would they go to find, seek, and eat them? Think about what is realistic or achievable, and then take that idea to the extreme.

- **Puns.** Are there words that sound like/look like/have a similar meaning to words that relate to your brand, product, or industry? Can you play around with them to put a new spin on their meaning?

- **Create lists of three, whenever you can.** After listing or grouping two things that are alike, create a third that is unexpected or surprising.

Want to learn more about comedy?

When I look back on my comedy journey, there are several books that stand out as having had a huge influence on me, inspiring my early learnings and understanding of what comedy is and how the industry works. If you want to learn more about comedy, here are a few that I've used, which I highly recommend:

Be a Great Stand-Up, by Logan Murray

[The] Bedwetter: Stories of Courage, Redemption, and Pee, by Sarah Silverman

Born Standing Up: A Comic's Life, by Steve Martin

[The] Cheeky Monkey: Writing Narrative Comedy, by Tim Ferguson

[The] Comedy Bible: From Stand-up to Sitcom – The Comedy Writer's Ultimate "How To" Guide, by Judy Carter

[The] Comic Toolbox: How to Be Funny Even If You're Not, by John Vorhaus

Finding the Funny Fast: How to Create Quick Humor to Connect with Clients, Coworkers and Crowds, by Jan McInnis

How to Write Selling Humor, (audiobook), by Peter Mehlman and Mel Helitzer

Seinlanguage, by Jerry Seinfeld

Seriously … I'm kidding, by Ellen DeGeneres

Step by Step to Stand-Up Comedy, by Greg Dean

 ## Don't forget

- Humour is one of the most powerful ways to connect with others.

- Comedy is an art form accessible to all. The rules, formula, and structure can be learned and applied by anyone.

- Even if someone has never heard of your brand and doesn't use your product, if you make them laugh with a video or image online, they'll connect with you.

- When we laugh, we're engaged and 'in the moment' which, in today's age of digital distraction, is an impressive achievement.

- Forms of humour include observational, sarcasm, deadpan, self-deprecation, parody, irony, satire, puns, slapstick, and blue comedy.

- Strategies to get funnier with your content include: the rule of three; exaggeration; and adapting common references, like clichés and stereotypes.

- Comedy is subjective – you'll never win everyone over with the same piece of content or comedic style. But by all means, try. (I've been trying for 105 pages so far.)

Chapter
10

STAY TRENDY:
POP CULTURE AND
NEWS AS INSPIRATION

Whether you're a 20-something social media junkie who knows what One Direction wore to the Grammys or your idea of up-to-the-minute highlights is the latest interest rate rise, popular news items are a great source of content inspiration. By tapping into the conversations people are currently having online, combining a news item, event, or theme with your content is a fun (and often funny) way to drive discussions with customers that fall outside of your normal conversation sphere.

Some obvious targets for jokes and parodies are celebrities and reality-show contestants, but there is no limit to what you can use as inspiration. Anything and everything that demands our attention is a potent and potential source, including (but not limited to) politicians and their campaigns, sports teams/athletes and their dramas, and celebrities and their divorces.

Pop culture and trends

Trends in fashion, food, and the internet, as well as movies and TV shows with cult followings, are rich sources of inspiration. Think *Star Wars*, *The Hobbit*, and *True Blood*, as well as classic sitcom characters like Homer from *The Simpsons* or Kramer from *Seinfeld*.

If your content appeals to your customers' interests and passions, not only will it show them that you're a brand that's hip, but you'll impress them in an unexpected way. By connecting the dots between your product or service with something that's meaningful in your audience's world, you create an additional connection beyond the one you've already established to your product or service.

Famous titles, classic characters, popular one-liners

Similar to the way we discussed putting a funny spin on clichés in the last chapter, popular movie titles, classic TV shows, favourite one-liners, hit song titles, famous characters, and even superheroes are a great source of fun content inspiration. Replacing words, adapting famous phrases, and using pop culture concepts as themes in your own content can appeal to a wide audience and cater to people's passions.

Consider some well-known quotes from movies. Can you think of any ways in which you could adapt famous quotes to promote your product or service? Or, can you think of ways to use a cult movie theme as an umbrella concept for your content? For example, your customers might not want to share a 30-second clip promoting your newest cordless vacuum cleaner. But if you create a short video advertisement that shows a blue-and-grey-coloured vacuum cleaner, with a yellow and black logo, swooping into three 'disaster' situations, saving people from stepping into tornados of mess, they might be more inclined to share it, especially if it had a Gotham-like backdrop and a superhero-style backing track. I know I would. Particularly if you time it around the next big *Batman*-related release.

A note of caution: just be wary of straying into the plagiarism minefield. When in doubt, check it out – *before* you publish and publicise it. A quick consult with a copyright-savvy lawyer could save you major headaches and expense later on.

So, open your eyes and start seeing the world around you with a different filter because you'll find inspiration everywhere – inside magazines, among your DVD collection, scrolling down your Facebook News Feed, or right next to you as you walk down the city streets on a Sunday afternoon. These pop-culture and current-affair doses of content inspiration can directly influence heaps of content: podcasts, how-to guides, newsletters, lists, memes, videos, infographics, and more. Whatever makes people buzz can be used to create content to help your brand buzz online.

Captures My Attention: Mashable's Miley Cyrus Wrecking Ball

One of the best pop culture-inspired content ideas I've seen was a stellar recreation of Miley Cyrus and her famed wrecking ball. In case you don't remember all of Miley Cyrus's controversies, I'll fill you in one of the most memorable. Back in 2013, when the pop star released her incredibly successful single 'Wrecking Ball', the former Disney darling unveiled a super-racy clip to go along with it.[64] In the flesh-heavy video, Cyrus can be seen bashing down walls, suggestively licking a sledgehammer, and straddling a giant wrecking ball, all while virtually naked. Cyrus is provocative and destructive in the video, which, unsurprisingly, attracted outrage, praise, and parodies. Plus heaps of views. We're talking 100 million views in the first six days.[65] Massive! Fans and critics worldwide spoke about it, reacted to it, and mocked it – incessantly.

My favourite content-related response to this video was delivered by social media editorial giant Mashable at the South by Southwest 2014 festival, an annual music, film, and tech event held in Austin, Texas. Inside their 'Mashable House' display, Mashable recreated the scene from Miley's music video with a huge Mashable-branded wrecking ball for people to swing on.[66] Those brave enough to saddle up plastered pics across their social channels, tagging the images with #sxswmash. They set up a win-win scenario with an innovative and incredibly creative idea, cleverly using an online viral monster to inspire a fun offline creation that itself transformed back into killer online content. SXSW attendees could boast to friends about having ridden this hilarious never-before-seen Miley Cyrus-esque wrecking ball, and in the process Mashable received great exposure for their brand. Big claps.

Captures My Attention: Entrepreneur Barbie's LinkedIn profile

Let's turn the online-to-offline tables in the other direction. Just warning you: I'm about to drop a Barbie bombshell. Are you ready? It probably comes as no surprise that Barbie has a Facebook page, with more than 12 million fans.[67] But did you know that Barbie also has a LinkedIn profile? No, I'm not kidding. The page was built to help promote Entrepreneur Barbie, released by Mattel. Equipped with an iPhone, tablet, briefcase, and clutch, Entrepreneur Barbie wears a slinky pink dress and a diamond necklace. (As an aside, I've never run across any entrepreneurs who wear high heels at home. I run my own business and I've never worn a hip-hugging dress and diamonds during my Skype meetings. If I'm being honest, she's actually inspired me to want to wear more than just UGG Boots and sweats during the next conference call from my kitchen. But I digress…)

Back to the impressive part: Entrepreneur Barbie has more than 7000 followers on LinkedIn.[68] She doesn't post anything remarkable; in fact, the page really just promotes Barbie-related products. It's impressive because Mattel has chosen to use a business-focused social network as a means of bringing a plastic doll's story to life. In addition to giving extra merit to her corporate aspect, they're also exposing their product to thousands of people who would have otherwise assumed her career had peaked with Beach Barbie. While this LinkedIn page didn't influence me to buy Entrepreneur Barbie (although it might have influenced 12-year-old Jordana), it did make me think about how I could creatively use LinkedIn to promote my products and connect with my audience online in a way that makes them go, 'That's smart, that's funny, that's hilarious' – just like Mattel's page does.

So, what's next for the toy manufacturer? I nominate a LinkedIn page for Ken. I have a hunch he's going to reveal himself as a Cirque de Soleil performer, but don't quote me on that.

Real-time marketing: The Oreo classic

Jumping on-board news stories is an effective way to join big conversations. That's the essence of real-time marketing actually. Are you familiar with real-time marketing? It became a buzz concept after Oreo's now-famous 2013 Super Bowl tweet went viral. If you haven't heard about the great real-time marketing fairy tale, let me clue you in: when the power went out during Super Bowl XLVII, Oreo seized the moment by posting a witty Twitpic asking, 'Power out? No problem', and showing a single Oreo biscuit lit by a small spotlight, with the text: 'You can still dunk in the dark.'[69]

In the marketing world, this timely, fun, and distinctly relevant tweet became a monster success story. Often, posts by big brands can feel robotic, but this immediate, in-the-moment response made Oreo feel, well, real. This tweet wasn't automatically scheduled; the people behind the scenes at Oreo reacted, responded, and showed us they were actually *there*. Generating loads of online attention, this tweet demonstrated how powerful social media marketing could be when tied in with news and current affairs.

While a lot of real-time marketing is, by definition, reactive, plenty of effective real-time marketing involves extensive planning. By looking ahead on your calendar, you can plan and prepare smart, sassy, impressive content that ties in with popular news events and events we all celebrate, including classics like Halloween and New Year's Eve right down to the season closers of shows like *Mad Men* and *Girls*. There are plenty of entertainment and cultural moments that you can celebrate (read: exploit) with your customers.

Real-time marketing: Starbucks UK's royal baby Twitpic

One of my favourite examples of real-time marketing was a Twitpic by Starbucks UK celebrating the birth of the first royal baby.[70] In 2013, nobody knew whether the Duke and Duchess of Cambridge would be blessed with a little prince or princess, so many well-organised brands prepared both a baby blue and a baby pink version of whatever celebratory content they wanted to share online. I saw a lot of really smart and fun (and some awful) content but Starbucks UK nailed it. Their photo featured three Starbucks coffee cups: two regular-size cups and a baby cino cup. One of the cups had the name 'William' written on it, with a gold paper crown on top, and the other cup said 'Kate', with a silver tiara on top. In front of those was the baby cup, with a teeny, tiny gold crown atop. The text on the image read: 'And then there were three. Congratulations!' How adorable!

Starbucks' Twitpic was simple, sweet, and effective. It celebrated the huge moment with class, humour, and serious cute-factor. Best of all, by using its own in-store products, the photo acted as a trigger for Starbucks' real-world experience. No matter which Starbucks you go into, in countries around the world, you always get your name written on your cup. It's their thing. Granted, it's often inaccurate (I have been called Jorgana, Judyana, and Frank), it's a trademark step in the Starbucks in-store process. Seeing Will and Kate's names written on the cups personalised this royal baby image by providing a meaningful connection – and positive association – for Starbucks customers. Also, it didn't appear to have cost any money. Part of its charm was that it looked like it had been thrown together by one of the baristas, therefore bringing together the royals and the every-day man in a quirky, familiar, and relatable way.

The royal baby's birth was the perfect example of a news event that provided a great opportunity for brands to join a discussion that swept the globe and, in the process, flex their content muscles, promote their brand, and spread their key messages.

Exercise 10.1:

Use news and current affairs for inspiration

1. Visit a news or entertainment site, or look through your Facebook News Feed. What are the current big stories? What are people talking about? Find a story that grabs your attention.

Example: MTV Video Music Awards.

2. List the key characteristics that define this story. Start with the 5 Ws: who, what, why, where, and when.

Example: Celebrities; awards ceremony; rewarding industry leaders/ elebrating talent; Hollywood; every August.

3. What themes relate to this event?

Example: Fashion, music, tech, pop stars, talent, risqué activity, teen idols, voting, trophies.

4. Write down any links between items you have listed in questions 2 and 3 with your product/brand/service. How are they connected?

List as many connections as you can.

5. For some extra fun, list obscure ways in which your product/brand/ service connects.

Jot down three or four connections beyond what you listed in question 4. Consider both word and random associations. (Sometimes the more obscure your choice, the better.)

6. Which of those ideas lend themselves to online content? Think about your visuals, think about your voice. And make it fun!

If you're having a hard time finding something to connect with in today's news cycle, you can also seek inspiration from other creative work. Here are some ways to use popular music, TV, movies, and fashion trends to your content advantage.

Exercise 10.2:

Use popular creative work to inspire your own

1. First up, choose a movie, song, TV show, or pop culture theme or concept.*

2. Now it's time to create a link between the pop culture reference you've chosen, and your product or service.

a) Identify specifics in each of the following relevant categories. Choose details that people identify with the most.
  • Popular scene
  • Famous lines and quotes
  • Much-loved characters
  • Iconic moments/scenery/images
  • Character costumes and outfits
  • Lyrics

b) What are your product's or service's strengths? Write a list.

c) Now, create links between the items you've listed underneath points a) and b).

Hint: Can you (legally) adapt famous lines, lyrics, or quotes from a movie or TV show to your product or service? Can you create a meme for your brand that mimics a popular scene from a famous movie?

* Bear in mind that when it comes to copyrighted material, copyright infringement is a serious issue. Never use copyrighted material without permission.

Don't forget

- Popular news items are fabulous for content inspiration.

- What makes people buzz can be used to make your brand buzz.

- You can prepare for heaps of news, current affairs, and global events in advance, with a little forethought.

- Try adapting iconic quotes or cultural references to your brand.

YOUR BRAND: HOW TO GENERATE CONTENT IDEAS

The pressure to constantly create new content can feel daunting. Luckily, there is an abundance of potential content inspiration around us; it's just a matter of identifying and tapping into it. You never know what might spark a cool idea, so always keep an open mind. In the meantime, here are some ideas to help you generate content ideas.

Find new ways to package your content

Despite the pressure you might feel, you don't always need to create new content from scratch. Year after year we buy glossy magazines with the same features: 'Top 10 Ways to Lose Weight for Summer' and '10 Tips to Fit into Your Swimsuit'. It's often replica content from the year before, yet we keep buying it. Why? Because the glossy mags reposition their ideas in a way that makes us *feel* like they're fresh and new. By tapping into the latest health or popular fitness trends that matter to us *right now*, they make their content relevant to us. And you can do this too.

Take a moment now to look back at all the content you have generated, both online and offline. Look back at everything you've published, printed, or presented and ask yourself:

How can I reposition this, with a different angle?
How can I present this in a shorter and sharper way?
Is there a trend I can tap into?

This could involve taking the key points from a blog post and creating a hard-hitting slide presentation. You could take your favourite 15 seconds from a promo clip and create a short-form video. Better yet, you could turn your newsletter into a sweater. (Yes, I wrote 'sweater'. I just wanted to make sure you were still paying attention.) Sometimes, what you recreate is often better than the original, where you find yourself asking: *What was I thinking when I first made this?* Just like we all do when we look back at our Farrah Fawcett-style feathered flip from the '70s. Right?

Let's meet your senior executives

If you could ask the CEO of Coca-Cola one question, what would it be? Me, I'd probably ask him whether he secretly prefers the taste of Pepsi Max to his very own Coke Zero. There's exclusivity in getting access to the busiest person at an organisation. It's a cool concept, isn't it? Or how about the lead designer at Apple? Or the head buyer at Bloomingdale's? Whether it's a Twitter Q&A, a video series, or even a Google Hangout, it can attract attention and can go a long way towards helping you develop a deeper connection with your audience. (Plus, it shows there are real human beings behind the giant glossy logos.)

Captures My Attention: CPA's The Naked CEO series

One of the best examples I have seen of this is the award-winning campaign *The Naked CEO*,[71] run by Australian accounting body CPA Australia. Through a mountain of online content, including videos, articles, and exclusive interviews with senior executives at major companies, CPA's CEO Alex Malley doesn't just invite people to join him behind closed doors at CPA Australia; he also uses his seniority, reputation, and resources to offer valuable insight into other organisations. Malley interviews IBM's Managing Director (Australia), McDonald's Australia's CEO, the Managing Director of Heinz Australia… and the list goes on.

The Naked CEO puts the spotlight on the human side of accounting and finance, offering valuable insight and tips for the industry's up-and-comers. This series shows CPA Australia to be a company that's innovative, forward thinking, and up to date with trends that affect the emerging workforce. Plus, any team that can make the accounting industry interesting deserves a gold star.

Take us behind the scenes

It's often the things you don't think people will want to see that can be the most intriguing. If you have the guts to take us behind closed doors to create content that offers insight into your backstory, your values, and your staff, this can intensify your relationship with your audience. This includes the games you play during lunchtime, a photo of your whiteboard at the end of a brainstorming session, introducing us to your office pet, or maybe even a photo of your colleague fast asleep during a boardroom presentation.

That's why blooper clips at the end of a movie or TV show are arguably the best part: the deleted scenes, the outtakes, the gag reels. It's these moments that aren't perfect and aren't polished, when we see our favourite actors burst out laughing, or forget their lines, that we truly connect with. Bloopers are littered with mistakes, but they're honest, and they're the moments we love the most. So, take off your mask and show people your human side because your customers will connect with your honesty at a deeper level than simply skimming your weekly data reports.

Put your unique voice into a Q&A with your audience

A great way to generate content that you can guarantee your audience will want is by asking them directly. This exercise will help both of you. They'll ask you questions you might not have considered, and in return will (hopefully) get answers that will help their business. While this concept is not new, the way you package and present it can make your brand stand out. Plus it'll give you a fabulous opportunity to broadcast your industry knowledge.

Captures My Attention: #AskGaryVee

Author, speaker, and marketing genius Gary Vaynerchuk totally rocks his Q&As. He launched a YouTube video series in 2014 called #AskGaryVee[72] and his followers love it (myself included). Using the hashtag #AskGaryVee, Gary Vee calls out for questions on Twitter, and in each episode shares people's tweets, covering everything from social media strategy and entrepreneurial survival skills to the New York Jets and even dating advice. No matter what your knowledge base is, or where your marketing preferences lie, you can guarantee super-useful information is being served up. And best of all, it's delivered in the quintessential Gary Vee way. His manner is matter of fact, totally BS-free, and wildly entertaining. Even if the questions or topics don't impact you or your business directly, he'll woo you anyway, making you feel that everything that comes out of his mouth is the most important stuff you've ever heard.

Take a leaf out of Gary's book. Use your brand's unique voice and distinct point of difference to speak directly with your audience. It's a powerful approach.

Yet another Q&A tactic

Mike Stelzner, the founder of the *Social Media Examiner* website, also has a neat Q&A system in place for his 'Social Media Marketing' podcasts.[73] At the start of each episode, Mike invites people to record and send questions about social media and their business, and chooses one audio question that he plays back and answers. It's a great tactic that provides value, encourages engagement, and stirs some healthy competition with a school-like 'I hope he chooses me for the basketball team' attitude.

Ask your community for ideas

In addition to creating content that answers your customers' questions, you can also share ideas with them during projects to solicit their feedback:

Out of these logos, which do you prefer?
Which new lip gloss flavour should we launch: Mojito or Kahlua?
Should I eat the last chocolate donut, or would you argue that the first seven were enough?

Everyone loves to be heard, especially online, so ask away. The more investment your customers have in the lead-up to a campaign or product launch, the more invested they'll be when your product finally comes out – and therefore more likely to support it and share it with their network.

If you decide to go down this route, be prepared for all sorts of feedback, ideas, and suggestions to emerge: the good, the bad, and the utterly outrageous. It's like my stand-up comedy routine: when I invite the crowd to participate, I never know where the banter will lead. For that reason, I have to be ready to handle all sorts of situations. Make sure you're ready too, dedicating time to respond and engage. If people are going to brainstorm an idea with you, and for you, then please do them the courtesy of showing how much you appreciate their time and effort. Unless their suggestion is that you close up shop. Then you have my permission to completely ignore them.

Create your own killer case studies

Did Skittles launch a campaign that you told your friends about? Did you listen to a podcast twice because once just wasn't enough? If so, can you identify what it was about these content items that hooked you in?

Keep an eye out for content that attracts your attention because it could provide a good opportunity for a case study that you and your audience can learn from. In the exercise below I've included some of the questions I considered when putting my Captures My Attention case studies together for this book.

Exercise 11.1:

Create your own case studies

Pick a standout piece of content – a campaign, an interview, or a brand concept – that your audience can learn from.

1. What made it engaging? What are its strengths?

2. What are the key messages of the content or campaign?

3. How was it set up/structured? Why was that format suitable (video, blog, live interview, podcast, etc.)?

4. Why is it cutting edge, different, or better than what other brands are doing?

5. What are its advantages, its compelling aspects, in terms of voice and visuals?

6. Why do people connect with it? What emotions does it stir?

7. How can you apply what you've observed to content you create?

Get personal in an interview with an expert

An approach employed by plenty of podcasters, bloggers, and, of course, journalists, is interviewing experts. You can do interviews in person, on Skype, via email, or even on the telephone. Or, by the time you read this, maybe even via a Tupac-style hologram (like at the American music festival Coachella in 2012).

Choose someone who has achieved success in your industry and ask them about their journey, their advice, their ups, their downs, and maybe even their tips for removing red wine stains from white carpets. The interviewee's personal story will give you and your customers valuable insight, plus it will give the person being interviewed a chance to gain exposure in front of a new customer base. Likewise, if you create compelling content from their interview, they might share it across their network, which will give you exposure in return.

When you're interviewing, ask the basic questions that need to be covered, but also make time to ask questions you're personally interested in and passionate about. Ask questions you can't actually find the answers to in a Google search. It will make your content stand out, and it will make your interview richer and more memorable for both you and your interviewee.

In fact, I've taken my own advice in this book, as you'll see in Chapter 13. I interviewed creative thought-leaders who have personally inspired me along my creative journey. I was very grateful for their time and will be using the video, audio, and written content in a bunch of different ways: to create memes, blog pieces, and more. The sky's the limit (as long as you have the interviewee's permission, that is).

Having kicked off my career as a journalist, I've been interviewing people for what feels like forever. And I've made mistakes. Plenty of mistakes. So, I want to share some interview tips I've learned along the way that I hope will save you the post-interview embarrassment that I've felt on occasion.

Tips on interview techniques

- Research, research, research. The last thing you want to do is ask an interviewee whether they've ever visited Nepal when they've just launched a new book and TV series called *My Nepalese Travels*. Learn as much as you can ahead of time because they're giving up their time for you.

- Analyse the angles journalists and publications have used and be different. Don't do what's been done before, for your sake and for theirs.

- In addition to what you want to know, consider what fans and followers might want to know.

- Listen. Really listen. It's easy to focus too much on the questions you want to ask and in the process forget to be present in the conversation, to listen to what they are saying.

- Be open. The conversation might move in an unexpected direction. Run with it, if it's interesting. Sometimes the best discussions are the ones you don't plan.

- Always get your interviewee's permission before recording audio or filming the chat, and agree on how you will feature their content.

- Remember: your interviewee's time is valuable so make it count. And try not to talk much about yourself. It's their interview.

Quotes, quotes, and more quotes

We love quotes online. I don't know what the scientific rationale is behind why we are so drawn to quotations, but I can tell you from personal experience, and my quote-filled Instagram, Facebook, Pinterest, and Twitter feeds, that we love sharing these droplets of inspiration, moments of hope, bursts of reality – these sentiments that resonate with us. Yes, they can be annoying, but they can also totally hit the spot. Even if you're not a Photoshop aficionado, you can create your own designs using apps like Canva, Over, and Instaquote, to name a few. You can share other people's quotes or even originate your own memorable quotes. Nothing is stopping you. In fact, I should make that into a meme:

'Make your own memorable quotes. Nothing is stopping you.'

Jordana Borensztajn

Please note: For the full impact, please picture this quote hovering over a beautiful image of a pink and orange sunset featuring a silhouette of a woman with her arms raised in the air. See, it has impact, right?

Don't forget

- New content doesn't always have to be created from scratch. Reposition and recycle your archive content. (And it goes without saying that if you're repurposing other people's content, always give credit where credit's due.)

- Show people your human side – customers will connect with your honesty.

- Use your brand's unique voice to reach your audience.

- If your CEO is a fun-loving character with a larger-than-life personality, you're lucky – use it to your advantage and put him/her in front of a camera. If your CEO, on the other hand, is not a fun-loving character, consider keeping him/her behind the scenes.

- If your audience helps by brainstorming ideas online, thank them. They took the time. So should you.

- When interviewing an expert, ask questions you're passionate about – ones you can't answer by searching online.

Chapter
12

TAKING RISKS: FIGHTING CREATIVE FEAR

Have you ever had an idea that you haven't pursued? Can you identify the reasons why you didn't follow it through? Chances are it was a fear-driven reason. *What if my new business fails? What if the client doesn't like my design? What if people don't want to read my book?* Ahem.

It's easy to come up with dozens of reasons why we shouldn't embark on creative projects, and it's easy to listen to those voices of doubt, of scepticism. Fear is one of the biggest inhibitors to creativity. I personally have felt it more times than I can remember. *Can I do this? What will people think? Am I good enough? Will anybody even care?*

When it comes to online content, this fear can take hold in a massive way. Because online content is published and viewable for the www.world to see, it means that if we have an idea that goes belly up, we won't just fail in front of friends and family, but in front of strangers; possibly hundreds and thousands of strangers around the world. And thanks to screen shots, that failure might always stick around to haunt us. (Did I just scare you even more? Sorry.)

Finding the courage to see an idea through from conception to reality can be downright terrifying at times – but also exhilarating. As difficult as it seems and as gruelling as it feels to face our doubts, push past our fears, and take a risk, it strengthens us. It strengthens our character.

'If you hear a voice within you say, "You cannot paint", then by all means paint, and that voice will be silenced.'

Post-Impressionist painter Vincent van Gogh[74]

Fear vs. creativity

When exploring fear, and specifically how it impacts creativity, I have a lot to share with you. But I am also going to share some terrific insights from a professional who has a rich understanding of the psychology behind fear. Dr Steve Ellen is the Head of Emergency Psychiatry at Melbourne's Alfred Hospital and Associate Professor of Psychiatry at Melbourne's Monash University.

Dr Ellen explained to me that anxiety, stress, and the fear of failure can all impact creativity in negative ways. 'When you're really busy and you've got a lot of things on your plate, you get very anxious, stressed, and you worry – it's a version of fear. It makes you busy and it means you can't get that mental space to relax, take everything in, and let your mind do what it wants to do', he says.

When I asked Dr Ellen about the fear of failure, something we all confront, he said it can have an enormous impact on our creative aspirations. 'We always have a whole lot of things that we're wishing for, and a whole lot of fears about what will happen if we don't achieve them. "What will happen if I never achieve my career goals and I end up not being able to support myself and those I love?"

"What will happen to my dreams of success if I don't achieve what I want to achieve?" "What will happen to all the promises I've made people that I'm going to do this and do that?" All those thoughts go through our head, like a broken record. They stop us from being able to sit back, breathe, and get that space we need to let all the good things come in.'

Why is fear of failure so common?

When people fill out surveys about what makes them the most anxious, worried, and fearful in life, Dr Ellen says that the answers that commonly top the list include spiders, public speaking, death, terrorism, and fear of failure. 'The reason fear of failure is so inherent to being human is because it's the flipside of wanting to be successful. The flipside of wanting something is the worry about not achieving it. I just don't think you can have dreams and aspirations without also having fear.'

No matter who we are, or how we live our lives, we all have goals. Fear is an indication of just how important those goals that scare us are. 'We're naturally dreamers. Every generation is built up of individuals who want to be successful, which then progresses the whole society. We've all got dreams and aspirations – it's part of being alive. You could say that for animals with less-developed brains, theirs might be more basic ambitions, like to be fed, to be sheltered, to nurture their young: the standard biological ambitions of life. But for humans they're much more complex and multifaceted.'

So, what's the key to success? Here are three key takeaways from my conversation with Dr Ellen:

1. On managing big dreams and big fears:
   Dream big and break it down into bite-size chunks. Then break the fear down into bite-size chunks and overcome it, step by step.

2. On making big decisions:

Envisage each worst-case scenario, of pursuing vs. not pursuing your dream: trying and failing vs. being in the same place 10 years from now. Which possibility do you dread more?

3. On taking creative/career risks:

Think, plan, and weigh the risks. There is no magic answer. Only you can figure out what's best for you.

'I learned that courage was not the absence of fear, but the triumph over it.'

Revolutionary and former President of South Africa Nelson Mandela[75]

If you're learning, you'll never fail

As a long-term creative, experience has taught me that if you go into projects recognising that low points can be just as beneficial as highs, that's a strong mindset. If you stay true to your vision, even if you don't achieve your goals, you'll never truly fail because you're still moving forward, even if the path changes. I'm not saying that falling short feels good. Not at all! In fact, I would describe it as someone tearing your insides out and ripping your gut apart; *but,* the lessons you learn hold the power to inform and influence your future in fundamental ways.

Just ask some of today's most successful entertainers and entrepreneurs. People who have shaped the world around us attribute the lessons they learned while failing as pivotal in the pathways that led them to the success they're now achieving. In the tech, business, arts, and entertainment worlds, the creative work of artists and entrepreneurs like Oprah Winfrey, Steve Jobs, Steven Spielberg, Walt Disney, and Ellen DeGeneres will forever be used as benchmarks to inspire, influence, and inform future generations.

It's easy to look back on what these individuals achieved in an idealistic way, filled with awe and wonder. In hindsight, their journeys and successes often have a dreamlike quality to them. However, in reality, their road to success was often long, hard, and filled with plenty of potholes. Some of the greatest minds in this era failed – often multiple times – before they succeeded. Before Stephen King was the world's most successful horror author, before Walt Disney created a fantasy dynasty that changed the meaning of magic for children all over the world, and before Oprah Winfrey was in a position to give everyone free iPads, they, too, experienced rejection, just like the rest of us. Let's wind the clock back to reflect on the humble beginnings of a handful of influential artists and entrepreneurs.

Famous cases: They failed before they succeeded[76]

- In 1919, Walt Disney was reportedly fired from a newspaper in Kansas because he 'lacked imagination and had no good ideas'. I have two words for you: Mickey Mouse.
- Steven Spielberg was reportedly rejected at least twice by the same California film school. Oh, the irony.
- J.K. Rowling's *Harry Potter and the Philosopher's Stone* was reportedly rejected by 12 publishers before finally being accepted. Damn Muggles.
- After copping 30 rejections for his first novel *Carrie*, Stephen King was reportedly so frustrated that he threw his manuscript in the bin. Thankfully, his wife retrieved it and encouraged him to resubmit it. Carrie went on to become the first of a long line of best-selling thrillers. I still have nightmares from the clown in his thriller *IT*. You too?

- Oprah Winfrey was fired from a Baltimore TV co-anchor news position. Clearly the guy responsible for that decision blew his chance of ever getting a free trip to Australia.
- Steve Jobs was fired from Apple, a company he co-created. Perhaps you've heard of Apple?

In Steve Jobs' now-famous Stanford University commencement address in 2005,[77] he spoke about the ups and downs of his career. There are so many lessons we can learn from Jobs' inspiring path. One of my favourites is that everything happens for a reason because it turned out that, for Jobs, being fired from Apple was actually a blessing in disguise. In his speech, he told the students that in hindsight getting fired was a positive thing because rather than feeling the 'heaviness' of success, he instead felt the 'lightness' of starting anew, which opened the door to an unbelievably creative era in his life. He pointed out that his passion for his work provided him with the motivation to keep moving forward.

If *any* of these artists or entrepreneurs had taken no for an answer, or had chosen to give up on their dreams, they wouldn't have contributed to the world, and they wouldn't have changed the world. Their conviction in their vision propelled them forward, even when the people around them stopped believing in them. And it's because of their failures that they were driven to push themselves harder in their next endeavours. The low moments provided them with key lessons, insight, and experience that became integral in their journeys, paving the way to the triumphs we all applaud them for today.

'I have not failed. I've just found 10,000 ways that won't work.'

Inventor Thomas Edison[78]

Now, I would like to share a failure of my own…

Lil Jords: My failed attempt at rapping

Back in 2011, when I was working as a music journalist, I had a creative bombshell. It was a time when a large number of YouTube stars were emerging, so I created a persona of my own: a hip-hop alter ego named Lil Jords who rapped about celebrities. I had penned plenty of 'Roses are red, violets are blue' poems on my siblings' birthday cards so I was, like: *How difficult could hardcore, satirical rapping be? What do I need? A sideways hat, baggy clothes, and a bling necklace? Easy. I can almost taste the sweet, viral success!*

So I charged ahead, creating a YouTube channel, Twitter account, Facebook page, a dedicated Lil Jords email address, and purchased the URL www.liljords.com. Naturally, Lil Jords deserved a pimped-up platform.

I spent days writing rap jokes and researching synonyms, I bought heaps of crazy costumes, I spent entire afternoons in my audio producer's backyard studio, and even longer on my computer, editing my videos. I also worked really hard on my dope new 'homie' attitude. (That last sentence, specifically my use of the word 'dope', should indicate just how massive a failure this was.)

I rapped about Justin Bieber, Kim Kardashian, Lady Gaga, and more. I tweeted my videos to the celebrities in question and – lo and behold – Rihanna, Chris Brown, and Paris Hilton never responded. I made nine rap videos all up, which, on last look, attracted a total of 600 views. Only 25 people Liked my Facebook page and, yes, I was related to all of them. I think we can all agree my alter ego was far from a commercial success. A few months in, the truth hit me: Lil Jords wasn't going to get any product endorsements and she wasn't going to get millions of views. She was, categorically, a disaster – which turned out to be a blessing in disguise.

Over the past four years I've written, performed, and produced three solo comedy show seasons and I've hit the stage at world-renowned clubs in New York and Los Angeles. I have grown so much as a comedian that Lil Jords, circa 2011, is not what I would want to be known for, no matter how good I became at rhyming. Despite this video project being a complete failure, when I look back on it, I actually see past the bad outfit and fake gold teeth. The reality is, I'm happy to have tried – and failed – to make my alter ego an internet sensation. I had a vision for what I wanted Lil Jords to become and just followed my passion (apparently blindly, as evidenced by my costumes), exploring, expanding, and developing the concept along the way. In this failure, I not only learnt that people aren't interested in an Aussie girl with poor rapping skills, but, more importantly, I gained invaluable creative DOs and DON'Ts that have been fundamental in countless projects I've worked on since.

I didn't know Dr Ellen back in 2011 – and clearly I missed a few important considerations in my decision-making process – but I still managed to wade through the worst-case scenario. Well, I lived through it, actually, and came out the other side with skills that I still use to this day. When I watch these clips now, I cringe with embarrassment and can't believe I ever, *ever* thought that it was a good idea. At least I know that if I ever need a really good laugh, I have nine three-minute videos that totally hit the spot.

'Do not be embarrassed by your failures. Learn from them and start again.'

Entrepreneur, investor, and Virgin Group founder Richard Branson[79]

When performance anxiety takes hold

A pivotal point in creative endeavours is the moment you choose to share your work with the world. It's when you take your idea, your concept, and your creation – and all of the blood, sweat, and anxiety you've poured into it – close your eyes, suck in your breath, and hope for the best. Whether you're clicking 'publish' on a LinkedIn post, stepping on stage to deliver a speech, or simply introducing a new idea to a co-worker at the water cooler, it's the moment when you just pray that whatever it is you're offering is well-received.

This fear of putting ourselves on show is also known as performance anxiety. 'Performance anxiety is the anxiety we feel when we know we're under scrutiny. It's a very common form of anxiety, and fits under the general category of what we call social anxiety disorder', Dr Ellen says.

'It's when we know we're standing up and being watched, when we know people are judging our performance. We're married to our thoughts; we love our thoughts. We've put all this energy into creating what we're going up with, and we know someone is going to judge it. Fear of scrutiny and fear of performance and fear of being evaluated are just so significant. It really boils down to our fear of looking like a fool, looking like an idiot in front of people – not only the people we love but people that we don't even know.'

If you know how to manage performance anxiety, it can be a huge asset. Dr Ellen says that, according to the Yerkes-Dodson law, the more anxious you get, the better your performance gets. However, if your anxiety becomes overwhelming, it does the opposite: it inhibits your performance. 'For most activities, whether it's exams, thinking-related activities, sporting activities, creative activities, [anything] that involve performance, anxiety actually makes you more alert and makes you perform better, until you get to this critical point where your anxiety starts knocking your performance off, and then you start going down', he explains. 'The key is to get enough anxiety and enough arousal to be performing well without dropping off the other end and going backwards. The more you perform, the more you get a sense of where you are on the curve.'

Dr Ellen says that the thought processes involved in performance anxiety can also have a huge impact on us. 'One of the great fears is some horrible error that we've done, like "I've mucked up my science" or "I'm just not funny" or "This show just doesn't flow". We've got this deep-seated fear that not only might they (the audience) not like what we do, but that they might shoot us down in flames. They're the things that go through our mind; they're the things that eat away at us; they're the things that contribute to our anxiety.'

Are you ready for some good news? Or, rather, great tips? If fear has previously stopped you from moving forward, you can change that pattern. Dr Ellen provided some tips on combatting performance anxiety.

Tips from Dr Steve Ellen to combat performance anxiety

1. Practise

The number one way to overcome performance anxiety is to practise, practise, practise. 'If you get used to presenting in front of 10 people, then sooner or later you'll be able to go to 100, and then 1000, and then 10,000. It builds up. Also, you learn more and you get better at your craft, which gives you more confidence.'

2. Take care of your health

Look after your health, which includes stress levels, sleep, nutrition, exercise, and relationships. 'Try to not do too many things at once. If you go into a performance incredibly stressed, the performance stress will be like an additive. You have to get your basic stress levels under control.'

One important piece of advice, he says, is to sleep well, particularly the night *before* the night before. 'No-one ever sleeps well the night before a big performance so I always make sure it's the night before the night before. No alcohol, no going out, no nothing.'

Nutrition is also important, as is keeping fit and healthy. 'In particular, avoid stimulants before a performance. Coffee is a stimulant and it makes you anxious. Be careful about how much alcohol you [consume] because a lot of people use alcohol, especially for night-time performances, and it's risky. A little bit will calm you down but too much will take away your performance skills. You'll lose your edge.'

Also important are key things in our lives, like exercise and relationships. 'Exercise is just so important for your general health. It relaxes you. There is nothing better', he says. And, believe it or not, 'if you're not taking care of your relationships, you're basically having a crappy time in life, and so you need to address those as well.'

3. Self-help: Arm yourself with skills

Dr Ellen's third tip comes down to what works for us as individuals. 'Everyone has different tips and tricks. For some people it's hypnosis, for some it's meditation, and for others it might be a particular herbal remedy or a pattern of exercise. Some people can exercise away their stress, some people can talk it away. Find what's right for you', he suggests. 'Self-help in anxiety and fear is wonderful. There is so much that you can do, and there's so much that's easy to do by yourself, by educating yourself and learning which of the different tips and tricks out there work for you.'

4. Seek professional help

If performance anxiety is really getting in your way, Dr Ellen recommends professional help. 'I always say try self-help first but if not, seek expert help. There are a million professionals out there who deal with performance anxiety, mainly psychologists but a whole lot of others: GPs, hypnotherapists ... and they will teach you specific strategies. They teach you relaxation techniques, they teach you breathing techniques, voice techniques. They can train you up in all sorts of ways, either with or without hypnosis, and they can do wonders. Most people do really well.'

Dr Steve Ellen's tips

1. Practise, practise, practise

2. Take care of your health, including stress levels, sleep, nutrition, exercise, and relationships

3. Explore self-help: Educate yourself and arm yourself with skills

4. Seek professional help

'If your dreams do not scare you, they are not big enough.'

Liberian President and Africa's first female elected
head of state Ellen Johnson Sirleaf [80]

Zucker Up! It's the journey, not the destination

Throughout my career, I've battled a lot of fear. As a music journalist, I used to get nervous every time I interviewed a band that I loved. As a comic, I still feel a twinge of panic when an MC calls out my name. And when it comes to posting a new blog, a new video, or a tweet I've spent the past 10 minutes crafting, I still feel giddy the moment I push 'publish'. It's just part of my creative process.

When I look back on all of the situations in which I have felt performance anxiety, the scariest moment was during my *Zucker Up!* adventure. We've all heard the adage that the journey is more important than the destination, right? In case you have any doubts, it's true. You see, I've learnt something really valuable throughout my career as a social media comedian. I've learnt that through using a creative approach like humour, I can connect with complete strangers.

That made me wonder: If I can use the power of creativity, the power of laughter, to connect with anyone in the world, who would that be? Oprah? Jerry Seinfeld? Julia Louis-Dreyfus? No. I decided I wanted to meet the guy responsible for the years of my life I have procrastinated away on Facebook. So I aimed straight for the top: founder and CEO of Facebook Mark Zuckerberg. I know it might sound weird to you, but I really love social media. Plus, as soon as the idea popped into my head, I was, like, 'Imagine how much amazing online content I could create through this adventure!'

So I set myself one of the most unrealistic goals ever: a 12-day quest from Melbourne to Silicon Valley to find Mark. I wanted to make him laugh with my best Facebook jokes. I was, like, 'Imagine if I could meet Mark because of *comedy*. Imagine if laughter and creativity could connect me with a stranger who lives halfway across the world and happens to be worth more than tens of billions of dollars. How cool would that be!'

I was excited, terrified, and completely determined. Now, I knew I couldn't be 'just another tech fan'. I had to stand out. So I thought, how can I combine my love of social media with my love of comedy to create something that would grab attention that's never been done before? YES! I'll create a Facebook Like costume. Because who doesn't think dressing up as a giant thumb is cool? (Hadn't I learnt anything from Lil Jords? Why do I keep dressing up?)

I stopped at the Dallas Digital Summit and in New York City before finally arriving at Facebook's headquarters in San Francisco on day 10 of my quest. I documented my whole journey online with pics, videos, and blog pieces, and I made a bunch of new Facebook friends and fans along the way. But now that I had arrived, the pressure was really on.

I pulled up to 1 Hacker Way, saw the famous Facebook Like sign outside campus and I was instantly overcome with nerves.

Despite the hundreds of friends, family, and fans following my journey, I was alone. And I was petrified. Everything I had invested energy into – the entire quest – culminated right here. As I drove through the boom gates, I felt myself starting to panic. *What am I doing? Am I really here? Am even I allowed to be here? Is this private property? Help!* I picked up the one thing that could calm my nerves – my iPhone – and immediately checked in on Facebook with a status that didn't reveal any of the horror I was experiencing: 'I HAVE ARRIVED!'

I collected myself as best as possible and put my plan together. *OK, I'll put on my giant Like costume and just ask people to point out where Mark's office is. Californians are friendly, right?* I open the boot of my car, look down at my giant costume and I'm frozen. *I can't do this. They're going to hate me. Why did I come here? Am I going to get sued for copyright infringement?* The fear was overwhelming. I've been nervous during my comedy festival seasons – really nervous – but this was different. I wasn't scared that people wouldn't laugh at my jokes; I was scared I'd fail on my quest, and everyone following me would judge me. Big time. But I also knew I had no alternative. There was no turning back. I had told the world that this giant Like would succeed at any cost.

After 30 minutes of panicking, with shaking hands I unpacked my costume from my boot, and with a huge, deep, terrified breath, I somehow managed to throw it over my head. And it was like magic. Within moments of my transformation, staff were waving at me, smiling, laughing, and asking for photos, and I was told my picture was uploaded to Facebook's Intranet. I was ridiculously excited but still super nervous. I headed out to the huge sign and snapped some selfies, including my favourite photo to date, my giant Like costume in front of the giant Like sign. People driving past were tooting their horns, school buses with kids were cheering, and Facebook staff arriving on campus were laughing, and taking pics of me with their smartphones.

Things were looking great.

Just when I started to feel a little confident (for a thumb), out came a guy from communications. With a smirk, he said, 'OK, what's going on?' I told him about my quest and my goal to make Zuck laugh, and he smiled and shook his head.

'Look, Mark's away on vacation right now. And we have a really good relationship with the Menlo Park police, and they told us that a giant Like is a distraction to people driving past, so...'

I don't remember much after that because I blocked it out, but I will never, ever forget that moment: on the grass, in front of the giant sign, dressed as a thumb, thinking, *Oh my gosh, all this for nothing. I have failed.* It was time for me to pack up my enormous costume and move on and I was crushed. I knew that no amount of begging and pleading would change the situation; it might even have made it worse. I also had no idea whether Mark was actually away or if he just didn't like my Like. None of it changed the end result. I wouldn't get to see him, and I wouldn't get to tell him five minutes of Facebook jokes. I had failed in achieving my goal. I felt humiliated, ashamed, and devastated – so devastated. *What are people going to think? They're going to judge me. They'll say I'm a loser. I wish I never did this. I'm such an idiot.* It went on and on.

I went straight to Starbucks in nearby Palo Alto to eat my pain away (don't worry, I left my costume in the car) and skimmed over my images and videos from the past 10 days to see how I could possibly spin this disastrous turn of events in such a way that I didn't look like an idiot to the people who had been following and supporting me for the last 27,735 kilometres.

As I made my way through a Starbucks triple espresso and granola, I looked at the Facebook posts, the brilliant support from friends and followers which blew my mind, interviewing tourists at Times Square, giving away free Hershey's Kisses in exchange for Facebook Likes at Grand Central Station, laughing and connecting with complete strangers, and then the Dallas Digital Summit. I captured video messages of support from Apple's co-founder Steve Wozniak; CEO of Zuckerberg Media and former Facebook marketing executive (and Mark's sister) Randi Zuckerberg; AOL's 'Digital Prophet' David Shing; and even from Susan Bennett, the voice behind Apple iPhone's Siri.

In that moment I realised: *I haven't actually failed at all.* I set out to connect with people through creativity, by using laughter and sharing my passion, and I did it. I totally succeeded. The originality of my idea had captured people's attention. And this quest continues to be a success because it gave me the confidence to do so much more creative work afterwards. I sold out comedy shows, I run my own workshops, and I even wrote this book. So much of that stemmed from the experiences I had through *Zucker Up!*

The best part is that, when I finally went on Facebook and told everyone what happened, people didn't judge me. They were totally on my side. In fact, they thought Mark was the one who'd missed out, commenting:

'And so begins the downfall of Facebook (as seen on Facebook).'
'Can't he just Skype you from his private island?'
'Dislike… damn you.'

I learnt that getting a *yes* or a *no* from Facebook's CEO didn't actually determine the success of my quest. It was a success simply because I gave it a shot. I fulfilled a dream, going from Melbourne to Silicon Valley dressed as a giant Facebook Like. I survived driving on the opposite side of the road (seated on the opposite side of the car), plus, according to Facebook's site, it has more than 936 million social network users[81] and now its staff know my name. *Me!* This experience taught me that failure is nothing more than a matter of perspective: it's how you interpret a situation that truly determines whether you've won or lost.

OK, now it's time for a fun exercise. Actually, I can't guarantee it will be fun but I can be sure it's something you probably didn't expect to do today. We're going to dig through what you see right now as your past failures in order to uncover some golden lessons.

By failures, I mean anything you started, launched, invested in, created, worked on, or decided to do that you didn't finish, or that didn't finish in the way you'd originally envisaged. Have you been fired from a job? Did you launch a podcast that had a lifespan of only three episodes? Did you invest thousands into a product that failed? Yes? Excellent! We'll put all of these to good use.

Keep a list handy of all of these lessons and look back on them whenever you get new ideas.

Exercise 12.1:

Find lessons in your failures

1. List as many projects, business endeavours, career pathways, or personal life choices that you can recall that didn't end the way you'd intended.

2. Identify exactly why each item on your list wasn't a success.

Examine each. Why didn't it work? List its strengths and weaknesses. Pinpoint the moment things started going downhill. What happened? Why?

3. Outline what you would do differently if you could do it all again.

What would you change? Which decisions? Which actions? Which strategies?

4. Turn the negatives into positives: List the lessons you've learned.

If you can't think of any answers right now, don't worry. These are the types of questions and answers that will hit you in the middle of a gym workout, while you're cooking stir-fry, or even as you're drifting off to sleep. So, keep your notebook nearby. You never know when one of your failures will come back, not to haunt you, but to benefit you.

Also, don't cast judgement on any of the answers you come up with. Some people might have really specific answers, like, 'I shouldn't have given $50,000 to a business investor I met in the bathroom at the airport', or 'I shouldn't have hired a university student to edit my novel'. Or they might be more general, like, 'I shouldn't let fear stand in my way'. No matter what lessons and reflections you come up with, they're all valuable.

'It's only truly a mistake if you make it again.'

Entrepreneur and author Randi Zuckerberg[82]

 ## Don't forget

- Fear is an obstacle to creativity. It's easy to find reasons why we shouldn't embark on creative projects and it's easy to listen to those negative voices. Especially if they sound like your mother-in-law.

- If you stay true to your vision, you'll never actually fail, even if you don't achieve your original goals.

- Lessons learned through failure have the power to positively inform and influence our future. The greatest minds of our times have failed, often more than once, before succeeding.

- Tips to manage performance anxiety include:
  - Practise – lots of it
  - Taking care of your health (stress, sleep, nutrition, exercise, relationships)
  - Exploring self-help options
  - Seeking professional help

Chapter
13

INSPIRATION: INTERVIEWS WITH CREATIVE THOUGHT-LEADERS

A wide number of innovators and pioneers in industries I'm most passionate about inspire me and motivate me to take risks with my career and my creativity. I was lucky enough to interview a handful of key people in the comedy, content, social media, fashion, and speaking worlds whose work has impacted me; people I have learnt from, continue to learn from, and who I trust you'll enjoy learning from too:

- Judy Carter – Humourist, author, speaking and comedy coach
- Mark Malkoff – Comedian, filmmaker, writer
- Cameron Parker – Former Black Milk head of sales and marketing
- Joe Pulizzi – Content marketing evangelist, Content Marketing Institute founder, author, speaker
- Brian Solis – Digital analyst, futurist, anthropologist, author, speaker
- Randi Zuckerberg – Radio host, author, speaker, Emmy nominee, founder and CEO of Zuckerberg Media

These 'creative thought-leaders', as I describe them, are at the top of their game. While their areas of expertise, career pathways, and individual stories are markedly different, the characteristics they share include imagination, passion, character, and courage, leading them to break new ground in their respective fields.

In the course of these interviews, I came away with far more than I'd originally anticipated. We discussed their individual takes on what creativity means to them; its value, potential, impacts, and influences, both personally and professionally. This is unquestionably my favourite among all the chapters.

You don't have to be a stand-up comedian, author, speaker, analyst, filmmaker, or fashion leader to be creative. We are all creative in one form or another – if not in career, then certainly in life. So, sit back, grab a cup of coffee (or glass of Champagne, depending on your mood) and indulge in some of the highlights of amazing stories from people who have turned their dreams into reality.

Oh, and keep a pen and paper handy because, trust me, there are a *lot* of quotable quotes.

Introducing Judy Carter

Judy is an author, humourist, speaking coach, mentor, and comedy coach, who has broken tonnes of new ground in both the speaking and comedy worlds.* She launched the first comedy classes in Los Angeles, was featured on *Oprah* with her first comedy how-to book *Stand-Up Comedy: The Book,* and has helped hundreds of comic hopefuls look inside, face the unknown, and find, write, and share their debut five-minute stand-up set. Most recently, Judy wrote *The Message of You*, which encourages people to turn their life stories into moneymaking keynote presentations: to turn their 'mess into success', as she describes it.[83]

Judy is a creative thought-leader because she was one of the first comedians to successfully teach her craft, she constantly uses her talent and gift to help others, and improves and transforms the lives of clients, comics, and speakers daily, helping them grow and develop their careers while inspiring everyone around them.

Tapping her creative vein

'My entire career is based on creativity because I've never had a job. So, for people to pay me, I have to wake up in the morning and think of somehow or something I could do that people would pay me for', Judy says. 'My job, essentially, is to convince people that they need to be more creative; they need to be funnier – mostly business people.'

Over the years, Judy has helped hundreds, even thousands of comics craft their debut five-minute set to share with the world. Through her books and classes, she provides insight into how the creative mind works, inspiring students to tap into their own experiences and creativity.

---

* The first comedy lessons I ever learned were from Judy Carter's definitive guide to everything funny, *The Comedy Bible*. If you're tempted to delve into the world of stand-up, her book is a must-have, and will equip you with all you need to know about setups, act-outs and attitude.

'Most of us think in terms of the creative mind as our right brain. Yet, most people who are very creative – the Picassos, the great football coaches, the people who act on sheer instinct and creativity – cannot teach what they do. I am unusual in the way that I [can] not only build a sandbox but I know how to play in it, so I'm able to see structure in creativity, see formulas in it, which has been very helpful to people accessing their own creativity.'

Teaching stand-up

Do we all have the skills and ability to perform stand-up? 'Maybe for five minutes', Judy admits, laughing. 'I've taken people who were absolutely humour-impaired, found that one thing that made them angry, and taught them how to make anger funny, so they had passion. [They experienced] the thrill onstage of standing there and *not* being that person who cleared a room when they told a story, to *not* be the boring one, but instead to be that person who got a laugh. For some, it was the most thrilling rollercoaster ride of their lives.'

Stand-up comedy is scary for everyone. Judy never pushes people to fight their fears, but instead works within their comfort zones. 'Stand-up is something you can do only if you really, *really* want to take on a challenge. I don't help them overcome fear – alcohol does that for them! I only encourage people who really want to, or have a burning desire. It's very scary, so most people don't. Sometimes when I coach people, they'll pay my fee and never show up the second time. This whole thing of being honest and authentic and funny at the same time as letting down your defences and being vulnerable in front of people is quite scary.'

Fear

'Fear is necessary to make us human, and it's authentic', Judy says. 'If you're not scared, check your pulse.'

Turning ideas into reality

For a creative like Judy Carter, ideas aren't special. She has millions of them. When they hit, she dictates them into her phone, and from a list of 100 ideas that seemed brilliant at the time, there might only be a handful that, on reflection, are worth following up. 'There are so many people who sit in front of the TV and [exclaim], "I thought of this; it was me!" I thought, "Wow, I should write a whole book about thrones and the *Game of Thrones!*" So, ideas are nothing. They don't mean anything. It's your brain belching.'

It's what you do with them that truly matters. 'There are those who try to implement an idea, and fail and give up. And there are those who keep doing it, who are willing to get up at the crack of dawn to write it, to work on it, to rework, to rewrite.'

Persistence pays off

While passion is important, Judy believes persistence is what truly gets you places. It's what helped turn her first 'big idea' into a reality. Despite the huge success of her books, including as Amazon bestsellers, Judy faced an uphill battle launching the first one.

'That book was rejected by 59 agents – 59! The message was: "Nobody's interested in learning how to do comedy." I kept going and it was number 60 who said yes. I got a book deal and it was one of the most exciting times of my life because I didn't know what else to do. I had come off the road and I didn't want to do stand-up any more. There are people who have persistence and a need to give birth to their ideas. I have a need to create. It's irritating.'

She shakes her head. 'Some people look at my life and go, "Oh, my gosh, you just write funny things and you talk to people – you're living the dream!" Do you know what my life is? Fifty per cent is research, what's going on in the world, 40 per cent of it is marketing, and 10 per cent is me being funny. It's not just like, "Yay, I'm passionate!"', she says.

Taking the plunge

In the early '80s, Judy made a choice that changed her future. Despite being a headlining comic, she didn't enjoy the club life. 'I didn't want to tour any more and work in comedy clubs, where they got violent. It was crazy. I was so lonely and the audiences were so drunk – I just hated it. I never wanted to be a famous stand-up comic. I hated being recognised, I hated the grind of it', she says. 'I wanted to be home, to stay put. I think that was really daring of me. It was really scary. And my mum had died too, so that was a big deal. I just didn't know what to do with my life.

'I've never had a job, I have no job skills, so what do I know? I thought: I know how to do comedy. Let me see if I can teach it. I put a little ad in the paper – it was, like, 20 dollars – and I said, "Hey! Stand-up class!" I had a couple of friends show up and I did my first class. Then I did another one, then another one.'

What was originally a simple solution to pay the bills and put food on the table turned into a concept that helped shape her career. These were the first comedy classes in Los Angeles, breaking new ground in a highly competitive industry. 'There's a saying that I've lived by, that when a door closes, somewhere a window opens, and that window turned into the life I have now, one I'm so grateful for.'

Judy's advice: Do something different

'The ultimate creativity is a life you design for yourself. We all have choices on how to design our life, but we don't always realise that those choices are there. Sometimes, acts of creativity and the choices that we make are scary, but, boy, I'm so glad I made them.'

We learn the most from experiences where we choose to do things differently, she adds. 'If you're unhappy, shake it up. Change something. If you always climb steps starting with your right foot, lead with your left foot. Do something scary. Go out for dinner by yourself – go to a place you've never been before and ask someone, "May I join you?" I did that and had one of the best nights I've ever had. I met somebody different, and he was a nuclear physicist. It was a phenomenal conversation.' Do something unusual, she advises. 'Make a different choice because that brings different opportunities.'

Failure is part of the process

'When you're redesigning your life and trying things out, you've got to feel in your gut whether it's right for you. Some of the things I try don't work out, but failure is part of the creative process. If you're not failing, you're not trying.'

Success is helping others succeed

Judy continues to make an impact because what she does is so different to what anybody else is doing. For Judy, this difference comes as a result of doing what she loves. It's not something she sets out to achieve.

'I never think about being different – I actually think the opposite. I think about what's going on in the world and how I can help others achieve success. Because that's all business is, no matter what business you're in. If you create a product that is incredibly brilliant but nobody needs it, it's not going to help people – you're not going to sell it. If you write a book, and this book is all about you and your personal stories, unless it's brilliantly written, it's not going to sell a lot. It has to do with [asking yourself], "What is your gift to others?" That's just what I try and focus on.'

Judy says that in order to truly help people out, you need to listen. It's that simple. 'I'm always looking for the clues. Sometimes you say something and someone will start crying, or you can see in their eyes that they're talking about something that means a lot to them. So, I really listen. I listen so hard. And then I start picking up what they're all about, what their gift is, and what their message is to give an audience.'

Judy loves making a difference by helping others reach their full potential. 'I'm working to create a ripple effect in the world; to be a wake-up call for other people, and to help others to be a wake-up call – to help people find those stories that really resonate, and make a difference that way.'

Her advice to a younger Judy Carter

1. 'Floss.'
2. 'Put sunblock on the backs of your hands.'
3. 'Don't be scared to try something new. Get your ideas out there, because you can always make them better.'

My takeaway: Judy Carter

Judy's golden nugget of advice is to create meaning in your life and have an impact by sharing your gift to help others. That message influenced my entire book-writing process. Before our interview I asked myself:

- What are the best topics to include?
- Which stories would be the funniest to my readers?
- What will make me look good as a writer?

Thanks to Judy that turned into:

- What will add value to the experience I give my readers?
- What exercises, tips, and strategies can I share to spur others to immediately get creative?
- How can I pass on my creative experiences and insights most effectively?

Now, what questions can you ask yourself?

Introducing Mark Malkoff

If you haven't watched Mark Malkoff's hilarious online videos,[84] go and check them out. Right now. This comedian, writer, and filmmaker is nothing short of a creative genius. His ideas are innovative, hysterically funny, and well planned. Here are just a few of the video challenges he has undertaken, to give you a tiny taste of his mastery:

- Mark lived inside an IKEA store in Paramus, New Jersey, for a whole week.
- In *171 Starbucks*, he visited and ate something at every one of Manhattan's 171 Starbucks within a 24-hour period.
- To conquer his fear of flying, Mark lived on an AirTran jet for one month, and broke the Guinness World Record for most scheduled flights in a 30-day period.
- He asked more than 150 strangers to carry him from the bottom of Manhattan to the top to prove that New Yorkers are friendly, and made it 9.4 miles without once touching the ground.
- He raced a bus down 42nd Street on a kid's tricycle to prove how sluggish Manhattan buses are.
- In his *Apple Store Challenge*, Mark tested the limits of what Apple would allow in-store, ordering pizza, holding a romantic date, getting his phone serviced while wearing a Darth Vader costume, and even taking a goat into the store. What a legend!

What started as passion-driven adventure – making videos to entertain people – has developed into a profitable career pathway. Mark is a creative thought-leader because he has an incredible imagination, exercises loads of courage, puts in heaps of hard work to pull off his stunts, crafts them with expert storytelling, and is wildly innovative. Every video makes me think: *I wish I had thought of that!*

Curiosity as inspiration

'Creativity for me is a muscle', Mark says. 'It's sitting down with a pen and paper and being constantly aware of my surroundings, and trying to be present and observe what is going on around me.' A blank sheet of paper allows him to be led entirely by his curiosity. 'It's … what I find amusing and funny, and exploring and just seeing what I can come up with. I really just try to go stream of consciousness – what makes me laugh, what am I curious about – and just unleash.'

Mark admits that some of his video concepts are complete nonsense, but he insists that's all part of it. From a list of 50 ideas, he'll pursue the one or two he's most passionate about. Mark looks at his list and asks: *What on this page gets me excited? What do I feel compelled to do?* 'I personally like to try to pull stuff off on paper that seems borderline impossible to pull off.'

Living in one of the busiest, craziest, and most colourful cities in the world has definitely fuelled his imagination. 'Creatively, New York has been really good for me as kind of a blank canvas. It's constant inspiration for what I do. There's just something that really stands out about it and I've taken advantage of it in a good way.'

The Apple Store Challenge

In 2011, Mark created the hilarious video *Apple Store Challenge*. After observing people do wild things in Apple stores, he decided to see how far he could push their in-store tolerance. Mark succeeded in having a pizza delivered, holding a romantic date, getting served while dressed up as Darth Vader, and bringing a goat into the store – and, in the process, created a killer video that's clocked up more than 1.1 million YouTube views and attracted a buzz of media attention. 'If you take something that has universal appeal, like an Apple Store, and take a very unique point of view that's never been documented, which I did … it has the potential to reach a lot of people.'

Before he embarks on any video project, he does his research. This particular video involved months and months of planning. '[It] was a solid year of me going into Apple stores. I would talk to people [who] work there, off-camera, and say, "Conceivably, could you do *blank* in an Apple store?" I would [suggest] the most outrageous things I could think of and they would all look at me, and I could see them thinking. They would pause and [then] they would say, "I don't see why you couldn't do that." I would say stuff like, "Could I bring a goat into the store?" If I did this in any other store, I'd get in massive trouble.'

Mark insists on ensuring that everyone involved in his videos is happy with the end result. 'Humour at other people's expense works for some people, but it's not my thing. I just want people to be happy. I wanted the Apple people to be happy and they were. I'm never out to make anybody look bad. I don't like mean-spirited stuff. I had no idea when I did it if [Apple] were going to let me bring the goat in. It shows you how cool they are. The video makes them look great; it makes them look cool and hip, and I got a great video out of it. So we all win.'

The 171 Starbucks challenge

In 2007, Mark created the video concept *171 Starbucks*, his challenge to visit every one of Manhattan's 171 Starbucks stores in a single day. As a non-coffee drinker, the goal to buy and consume something from every single store was an enormous undertaking. His caffeine-filled quest was a success and attracted much media coverage, including interviews on CNN, *The Today Show*, *Fox News*, and more.

'I don't even remember [coming up with the idea], but I wrote: "Would it be possible to go to every Starbucks store in Manhattan in less than 24 hours?" I didn't know how many stores there were, but that intrigued me', he reflects. 'I would call up the store and go: "What are your hours?" Somebody would give me the hours of a store and I'd call back three hours later and they'd give me different hours. I was just obsessed with this thing … the curiosity took over.'

The video campaign required extensive planning, strategising, and physical training, and took a huge toll on his body. His passion for the idea helped push him through the difficulties. 'Safety is a big thing, definitely, but 171 Starbucks – there was nothing safe about that day. My body started to shut down at hour 12. I couldn't walk in a straight line because of the heat and the caffeine consumption. I was up for 27 straight hours, and I was in pain for days. It was just so much work, but I would never have gone through with it if my enthusiasm for that idea wasn't strong. I had no idea that I was going to hit all 171 stores. I had to hit one every seven minutes for 23 hours straight and I had to train on a bicycle for a month. And all it [required] was the enthusiasm for the idea.'

How storytelling lures us in

Every video Mark unveils is packaged and delivered with compelling storytelling elements. 'Storytelling is so essential to get people engaged', he says. 'At the same time you've got to be 100 per cent authentic. I really do try, in all my stuff, to [make] that evident.'

While Mark tries hard to achieve his video challenge objectives, sometimes falling short adds dimension to the story, as was the case with his quest to ask strangers to carry him the entire length of Manhattan. 'I would meet people that had never been to New York and they would say, "I hear New Yorkers are not nice." And it's not true. It was frustrating. I observe all the time New Yorkers giving directions to tourists', he says. 'I feel like the reason that video worked and got so much media attention is because there was a definite story with a beginning, middle, and an end. I really wanted to be carried the entire length of Manhattan – it's 32 miles – but I was only carried 9.4. It was the coldest day of the year and it took 19 hours, and I think if the weather was better I would have made it, but the video absolutely 100 per cent still worked and I was on *Anderson Cooper* and *The Today Show*. It almost made it more real and authentic that I did not make it the entire way.'

Mark says the dramas and obstacles he faced added to the impact of his *171 Starbucks* clip, including the incorrect opening and closing hours, and bribing people to open stores. 'You get those things and you use them for your storytelling, and it adds layers to the story.'

How Mark gets people on board

Over the years, Mark has worked with all sorts of big names and brands. A positive attitude is vital. 'I just try to be as enthusiastic as possible when I approach these people and entities. Credibility is good. I've worked for free for years. Occasionally I'll do stuff for free if I'm in love with it. When I did my Starbucks project, I went on a lot of TV, so momentum is good. I could go to places and be, like, "I was on these shows." And then every project, I was able to get a little bit more traction, a little bit more coverage. All that stuff helps', he says.

In one of his favourite videos, *Celebrity Sleepovers,* Mark persuaded 13 celebrities to let him sleep at their Hollywood homes. He slept in Justine Bateman's (*Family Ties*) tree house, he snuggled Camryn Manheim's (*The Practice*) Emmy Award, Lisa Loeb (musician) read him a bedtime story, and Kate Walsh (*Private Practice, Grey's Anatomy*) got cosy with him in her pyjamas. Despite not having known virtually any of these people before contacting them, he believes that his positive attitude and genuine enthusiasm led to more than half saying yes to his pitch. 'Celebrities are used to getting requests for autographs and photos. I write a decent email that is enthusiastic and shows I just want to have a good time. I just want to have fun.'

In the case of IKEA, it took two months to get the furniture giant to agree to permit him to set up house for a week in their Paramus, New Jersey, store. 'I was politely persistent.' Each week he tried a different approach. 'I'd say, "This is what I was thinking..." and "This is why I think it would work."' Being enthusiastic and politely persistent is why he succeeds.

Content that captures Mark's attention

'I think anybody that just thinks different, that's able to take an idea that's universal and put a unique spin or a slant on it – that's the stuff that probably attracts me online.'

What about his fans and followers? People, he says, connect most with the ideas they can best relate to, like his challenge to outrun a Manhattan bus using a kid's bike. 'I raced a New York City bus [down] 42nd Street for one mile while riding a child's tricycle, a Big Wheel. All New Yorkers can relate to how slow a bus is. And I won by two minutes on a child's tricycle. I beat the bus!', he exclaims, still excited by the thought.

'I love it when I can include people. It's a nice thing getting people engaged. They feel they're a part of it, and they truly are a part of it.'

The power of passion

'The only reason to do anything', Mark declares, 'is because you love it. You're going to hit roadblocks – it happens in everything – but if you love it enough, you will work through those things ... If somebody is new [to something], it doesn't matter if you're doing videos, if you're doing music, if you're doing comedy, it normally takes time to find one's voice, and that just comes from doing it. You have to practise, practise, practise to take your skill to [the] next level. There's no substitution for doing the work.'

His advice to a younger Mark Malkoff

'Relax. Don't get caught up in results so much. Be present. I just knew from a really young age that I wanted to work in this medium and was always pushing myself. I feel like it would've been nice to just relax a little bit when I was younger. I was doing internships from the time I was 18. Most people don't do it until later. [But] I don't regret it – I learned a lot, and I had good experiences.'

My takeaway: Mark Malkoff

Mark is living proof that even the most outrageous, wild, and crazy ideas can be turned into a reality when combined with passion and hard work. It's clear that no matter how difficult ideas might seem, we should never give up on the ones we truly love, because they're often the ones that resonate the most.

He also highlighted important ingredients for video content that hits, which I'll now always have top of mind:

Unique Point of View + Universal Appeal = Winning Formula

Oh, and the fact that, in New York City, you can take a goat almost anywhere.

Introducing Cameron Parker

Cameron was the head of sales and marketing at Black Milk when we carried out this interview. As discussed in Chapter 8, Black Milk is an exceptionally creative and innovative fashion brand. What started as a one-man project in Brisbane, Australia, has turned into a global presence. Driven by passion, creative director James Lillis started his leggings-loving community as a blog, with a storytelling focus. Today, storytelling is still the driving force behind the community of more than one million Instagram followers[85] and 696,000 Facebook fans.[86] Their loyal communities are made up of diehard Black Milk advocates (Sharkies, as they're affectionately called) who love the brand, love the leggings, and love the friendships they've formed with each other.

Black Milk uses storytelling at every point in its customer journey to create an unforgettable experience. In both the fashion and social media spaces, Black Milk is a creative thought-leading company that creates a one-of-a-kind adventure for its customers. Cameron spoke enthusiastically about the ways in which Black Milk makes its customer experience so special, as well as the magic behind building and fostering a thriving community that unites over passion, nylon, and cool designs.

Brand storytelling: Buttering their bread

Black Milk would not be what it is today without storytelling. Cameron said it's been a fundamental part of who they are as a brand. 'That's the one thing that is in the heart and soul of Black Milk because it actually started as telling stories.' The brand, he said, before it even was called Black Milk, started with its blog, *Too Many Tights*, the first blog dedicated solely to legwear, tights, and fashion.

Black Milk still tells stories today, in countless ways. 'The shipping confirmations, the signing up – absolutely every point of communication we have with our customers is a story. We don't send an invoice – we actually tell a story. Each product doesn't just say, "Here's purple galaxy leggings". It's the story – and it's one or two sentences. Every collection has a new story.' Cameron said that storytelling always came naturally to its owner. 'James is a very good storyteller with a beautiful writing style. We were lucky. It wasn't something we strategically sat down and said, "We need to tell a story today". It was very organic. It wasn't forced, it wasn't contrived.'

As the brand has grown, the team that puts their stories together has also grown, with more strategy behind their marketing. The major difference is that now the brand uses social media to bring its tales to life. 'Every social media channel has its own role. And part of the brilliance about us is that we are vertically integrated. We can tell a story really easily and beautifully – from the creation of the idea through to the design team, through the creating of the actual garment, through the sewers and the cutters. And you'll see that through social media and the podcasts', he explained. 'We are very open. We're not protective. The brand becomes like an onion, and there are characters within it – like James, me [at the time], the mega hotties, the customer service team. And [there are] other characters in the business who we bring to life through social media. It makes the brand extremely relatable so customers can build actual, genuine relationships with us rather than very transactional [ones].'

Black Milk's brand of creativity

In a company that's released leggings that feature everything from *Snow White* and *The Little Mermaid* to Hogwarts and The Riddler themes, it's definitely creativity that keeps their world of leggings spinning. In terms of how much value they place on creating new ideas, Cameron said it's a daily, even hourly focus. 'With social media marketing, you've got to just be ahead of the game. No one is an expert. Every minute, every day, every hour, stuff is forever changing. We've got a global customer base so everything from the design to what we do as a brand is changing hourly, and daily.'

Where do they get their wild ideas from? It's extremely diverse, he said. They don't follow seasons or fashion trends. Their idea generation is internal. More important, it's through the customers. They listen to social media and their customers, their 'Sharkies', who are 'very vocal in terms of saying what they want and don't want'.

'We don't have a traditional fashion model that dictates what you'll be wearing. The roles are reversed ... we listen to our customers and they tell us what they love to wear.'

Millions of ideas are shared across their social channels. Social media, he explained, is their chance to record those ideas and identify trends so that they can tell their designers and pattern makers, 'Sharkies are loving this, and they would love this, and we'll change this pattern. There is constant feedback.'

Behind the scenes glimpses

Like any fashion brand, Black Milk does a lot of self-promotion. Because of their creative presentation and rich focus on storytelling, their posts never feel sales-y. Instead, they always feel inclusive, trendy, and extremely likeable.

'We're really conscious not to make it look like ads, in the traditional sense, or marketing, and that's why a lot of what you see on social media is user-generated content. Because it's real. It's not manufactured by us. It's manufactured by you guys. I would probably say nine [out of] 10 posts are on that. And when it comes to our stuff, it's very raw. "Here's James using the design room, whipping up some ideas", or "Here's the graphic designers and this is what they're working on". It's not polished, it's not fake, it's not forced. It's an awesome picture that we love, and a caption, and nothing more complicated than that. And the Sharkies love it.'

Offbeat

Nothing about the way Black Milk operates is usual, or expected. Their greatest strength is what makes them different. 'For me, as a [now former] marketer in this role, it's not traditional. I'm sitting here planning and thinking, "What fun stuff can I do?" I don't know if you've heard of Bounce, which is a trampolining company. I'm constantly looking at fun things I can do to connect people and I'm, like, "OK, let's do an awesome Black Milk event at all these Bounces across Australia. You have a big night where you wear Black Milk and get in for free. Like, 120 people wearing Black Milk and jumping around trampolines."'

Building offline communities

In addition to their thriving social media communities, Black Milk connects Sharkies offline via conventions and meet-ups right around the world, from New York, Canberra, and Toronto, to Warsaw and New Zealand.

Moving from the online world to the real world has made their brand even stronger, Cameron said. 'Some Sharkies are best friends and have formed really strong relationships. From a marketing [stand]point, it makes great sense, because these evangelists are very tied to the brand, and loyal. That loyalty is extremely strong.'

Cameron said that the real-world interactions with Sharkies deepen and strengthen all of the online connections that have been built. He said that he especially loved hearing about the positive and significant difference Black Milk and its community makes on the lives of its members. 'We're lucky', he said, 'because being fashion and youth, they actually do want to hang out ... it's great, and we do nurture that. I think the "pinch yourself" moments come when we go to these meet-ups, or I get an email, I get a letter, [when] someone has taken time to write a story about how the Black Milk community ... has had a positive impact on their life. When I go to meet-ups, there have been stories where maybe a Sharkie's husband has passed away and the first people to her door, or on the phone to offer help with the kids being picked up from school, or bring around food, are people she's met online.'

Showcasing their customers

If you search for Black Milk Clothing's hashtag #blackmilkclothing on

Instagram, you'll find hundreds of thousands of results. Countless photos are posted onto their Facebook page. Cameron said, when they can turn the tables by showcasing their Sharkies' pics, it's just as much fun for them as it is for the customers in the shots. 'For them to be reposted by [Black Milk] is like their mission in life. They're so excited. It's their five minutes of fame and that's why we do little competitions, and stylings, and have fun "pants-off Friday". Social media is like a party: we play our music and if you don't like it, whatever. This is the music we play.'

Taking risks

In order to stay at the top of its game, Black Milk needs to constantly reinvent the wheel, which means taking risks, all the time. 'Every collection is a risk. We work in fashion, so you are only as good as your next collection. Every day we've got the challenge to design better, cooler, more amazing gear, so we've constantly got to take risks and be innovative and creative. With social media and creativity, if you don't take risks, you are yesterday's news.'

What pushes them to constantly create and take these risks? Why not rest on their laurels? 'We've got this amazing passionate community out there, hungry for it, that's supporting us and backing us, and we don't want to fail them ... Everyone is going to have a personal taste, but generally [we want them to] walk away and go, "Oh, my God, I have to have that!" The passion and excitement – *that* gets us fired up; when our community is so excited about a release, and can't wait to get their piece from something that we have shown online – a sneak peek – that gets us fired up to continue doing more every day.'

Social media helped it happen

Cameron said that when he thinks about where the small Brisbane-based brand began, and where Black Milk is today, he is really proud of their journey and having been a part of it. 'Everything was against us in terms of manufacturing in Australia, selling online, being in fashion and trying to market something to the world which we had no money to do', he explained. 'If it wasn't for social media, I wouldn't even be talking to you today because we would never have had a channel that was cost-effective to promote us. So, if you can leverage that, the opportunities are endless – also, not being safe, not being mass. It was about a niche and forming a tight-knit community.'

His advice to a younger Cameron Parker

'It's a difficult one because if we didn't make all of the mistakes that we made, we wouldn't be who we are today. We've made mistakes but we've all learnt along the way. With all the social media it's, like, "Try it out. You'll soon know if it works or not." And I just love that. We've made mistakes, and we'll probably make another mistake tomorrow. You're going to make mistakes, and every time we have, we've learnt from it and grown stronger.'

My takeaway: Cameron Parker

In order to stay ahead of your game, in business, creativity, and in life, risk-taking is essential.

Passion and a strong community are essential for brands to thrive online. So, don't be afraid to connect with your audience. Be open and authentic and create meaningful connections and conversations.

And where and whenever possible, make time to meet your customers in real life. Think of your community as family. But not a dysfunctional family – a cool family!

Introducing Joe Pulizzi

Affectionately called the 'Godfather of Content Marketing', Joe is the founder of the Content Marketing Institute in Ohio, the author of multiple influential content marketing books, he speaks at conferences all over the world, and he is a huge online influencer.

In March of 2007, Joe left a highly paid corporate role to launch Junta 42, a company that sold content marketing services to agencies. Despite offering high-quality services, the financial model was fraught. Rather than give up, Joe changed his focus to education, training, and consulting and in 2010 set up CMI, the Content Marketing Institute. CMI is now the industry's leading educational resource for content marketing and runs the industry's biggest annual content marketing event, Content Marketing World, in Ohio.

Joe is a creative thought-leader because, throughout his journey, he has pursued his passion, followed his gut, maintained a strong conviction in his vision and every step of the way has used his insight and experience to share his knowledge with, and help, others. As a result he has become a pioneer and unbeatable force in defining and shaping the content marketing industry as it evolves.

Start small and find your sweet spot

In an age of nonsensical videos being viewed by millions, coupled with our need for instant gratification, Joe's insight on starting small and growing big is sound advice: 'If you want to be the leader in your industry, if you want to be followed, if you want to build an audience, you have to pick a niche that is small enough [where] you can be that voice.'

Joe's advice on finding what he's fond of calling 'your sweet spot' is to choose between what you know and are passionate about, and what your audience's needs are and where their passions lie. Viral content does not make a business. 'It doesn't happen in viral; it happens by infecting a few', he explains. 'And once you infect a few, that goes on and on and on, and grows, and now you have a substantial audience. That substantial audience could be three people depending on what you're trying to do. It could be one, actually, depending on what you're trying to do. And it's not difficult to do that.'

There is a misconception, he says, about the power of zeroing in on the pain points and informational needs of a small audience. 'Most people don't go in that direction because they feel they're limiting business options by going that small. I'm saying, "If you go bigger, you become irrelevant. Smaller, you become relevant." Let's become relevant. You can always go bigger. You can never go smaller.'

Connecting and core values

When it comes to role models, Joe gives his grandfather, Leo Groff, credit for a lot of his core values. Despite being in a different position to his grandfather, who was an embalmer at a funeral home, Joe says he learnt fundamental lessons about business connections from his grandfather that have remained with him throughout his career.

'It's an interesting industry. You have a lot of people … grieving and it's a very important, needed service. My grandfather had some failings, but what he did better than anybody else was [to treat] people like they wanted to be treated – with dignity and respect. And I saw that every day, growing up', he recalls. 'It's hard for that to not rub off on you. My greatest hero was my grandfather, and watching him do that, that's an art form, and that's how he grew his business – by just being a human being.'

Creating meaningful human connections is, and always will be, the key to success, Joe says. That's one of the things he loves most about today's social media and content environments. 'You [can] actually make a business out of that today; you can just be yourself. I really believe it's just having the mindset and mentality [to] believe that it's possible to do that; to be yourself, be passionate about something, and to take your passion and put that into something that you can monetise.'

Doubt isn't a bad thing

Joe experienced a healthy dose of doubt during his entrepreneurial journey. 'I was questioning my thinking every minute of every day. I was fairly confident that, if I had to, I could go find a job and support the family – I just didn't want to be depressed the rest of my life because I'm not built for that environment', he explains. Launching Junta 42, he says, was 'the greatest thing ever. Of course every entrepreneur thinks their idea is the best, and when you figure out after two years that it was not a great idea, or it could have been a lot better, then [with your] next idea, you're starting to question whether or not that's going to be a good idea.'

Looking back, Joe identifies a six-month period in 2009 when he was 'bleeding money', as one of his lowest points. *I'm two and a half years into entrepreneurship*, he thought. *I can't work for anybody anymore.* At that point, he didn't know what he was going to do, so he decided to stop feeling sorry for himself and said, 'OK, let's give it another six to nine months.' And that, he says, made all the difference.

In terms of what advice he would give to other entrepreneurs when they find themselves in a rut or a low point in their journey, he says to have patience – patience and grit. 'Grit's a great word. Something in the nature of "How do you battle through, when everything is telling you that you should give up?" Now, as I'm talking to other entrepreneurs that have made it – in [the first] three years, you're just getting started. I would say that most entrepreneurs that I know, that I'm friends with, who pack it up and pack it in, don't have a long enough timetable.'

Despite achieving CMI success early on, Joe says it wasn't until Content Marketing World 2011 that he really knew they were on to something special. 'I was always in a state of doubt that this was just a little hobby that tomorrow was going to be gone. Then I was out front, onstage, in front of 600 people [who had] paid a lot of money to be at a conference in Cleveland, Ohio, of all places, and they showed up and I'm, like, "We might have something here. This might actually work!" So, that was sort of "the moment". I didn't set the date that that was going to be the moment', he adds. 'Honestly, as we do new launches within CMI, I still think that way.' Entrepreneurs should always question themselves, he says. 'It's natural.'

Making mistakes

Like many entrepreneurs, Joe made plenty of mistakes. 'I make mistakes every day. Often a day doesn't go by where I don't make multiple mistakes. If you're not making mistakes, you're probably not trying hard enough, let's put it that way. The business model of launching into 2007 with Junta 42 was, in hindsight, a terrible financial model. I can't even believe I did that, but I can't totally fault it because from Junta 42 came the Content Marketing Institute and that model works really, really well. I don't know if I could have gone directly to CMI. I think I had to go through the desert, as some people would say, to get to that point.'

Hindsight makes a big difference, he says. 'I have a much more positive view of mistakes now than I did back in 2009, when I thought we were going to lose the business. Now, I can look back and say, "Wow! Those were some pretty good mistakes that you learned [from]. I wonder what mistakes I can learn from today." That's how I look at it.'

On not having all the answers

Despite being a pioneer and coining the moniker 'content marketing', Joe feels he still has much to learn. He keeps an open mind and a thirst for knowledge, and always gives credit where credit's due. 'I want to be the least intelligent person in the room', he declares. 'I want to be the one asking the questions.

'I am not a content strategist', he admits. 'I don't know everything there is to know about content marketing. There are hundreds of incredibly smart people [who] understand the practice area of content marketing better than I do.' And it's these people that

CMI brings to the table to help educate and inspire their massive community, through sharing their knowledge and expertise.

This 'shared knowledge' approach is a driving force behind CMI and is responsible for much of its success. 'Content Marketing Institute was started as a blog, so in essence it was started as more of a sharing platform. The thinking behind it, the reason why CMI exists, is there are a lot of smart people out there. We don't have all the answers, [but] we're going to help get the people who know the answers and put them on this platform [so that] we can all learn from each other.'

Keep setting goals

As a successful entrepreneur, goal setting is a priority for Joe. 'I feel there always has to be a new goal, so we never ever reach the finish line. If [you] reach the finish, you're done. You're actually done. Put a cork in it. Forget it. So, you've got to keep adding an extra 100 metres on there to see where you're going to go.'

Given his packed schedule, I asked Joe how often he redefines his goals. He writes everything in a Moleskin diary, he says, to keep his life on track. 'I look at my goals at least twice a week. I have all my goals in there; I have financial goals, family goals, spiritual goals, philanthropic goals, and I've had them for a long time. I haven't adjusted them much but I do adjust on occasion. I read them all the time. I actually take them on the road with me. When I'm on an airplane, and I have no electronics with me whatsoever, I sit for 30 minutes with those goals, just to make sure I'm doing the right thing: "Am I on the right path? Am I living a good life? Am I doing what I can for my family?" I can't tell you how important that is. And actually writing them down. Writing, for some reason, means more commitment to me than typing. So I do a lot of writing and sketching and drawing.'

Having a long-term plan and lots of patience are incredibly important, he advises, as well as aiming to make a small impact each and every day. 'The failure of people doing content marketing is always because they're either 1) inconsistent with the content, or 2) they didn't give it a long enough time. So I'm always out there just preaching patience, patience, patience. Don't go for the home run. Let's not go for the big hit. Let's go for singles and have an impact on our customers every day. That's where we'll see, over time, we'll make an impact – instead of doing it one at a time and just seeing if we can get lucky.'

His advice to a younger Joe Pulizzi

'My first response is … to not answer, because part of me believes I'm where I'm at because of the "bad" choices I made. That said, I'd tell him to target an audience that actually has money to spend, because the initial audience we targeted were agencies. And agencies are the cheapest people on the planet. If they have money, which they mostly don't, they don't want to spend it on marketing. In hindsight, I'm thinking, "What were you thinking, Joe? How could you actually create a business model that was based on getting money from agencies? That was the most ridiculous thing ever!" But that's what we did … And everything else is hard to say because it's a journey.'

My takeaway: Joe Pulizzi

More than ever, being ourselves in business can be one of our greatest assets.

It can take longer than one might think to get an entrepreneurial project off the ground – often several years (a concept that I find both comforting and stressful).

Joe's experiences prove that to truly succeed, you must keep revisiting your goals. Never settle, because you can always achieve more. And when it comes to content goals, don't focus on going viral, but, instead, focus on infecting a few that really matter. Like you.

Introducing Brian Solis

Brian Solis is a digital analyst, anthropologist, futurist, author, and speaker. As a principal analyst at Altimeter Group, Brian trains business leaders to understand the impact of disruptive technology trends and how to adapt to, and take advantage of, digital changes.[87] He delivers the kind of keynotes where I get frustrated because I can't tweet about them fast enough. To me, he is the Yoda of the digital world.

Brian has authored a number of highly influential business books, written articles for high-profile magazines and newspapers like *USA Today*, *Wired*, and *Fast Company*, he hosts an online video series focused on tech trends, he's the executive producer and host of the annual Pivot Conference in New York ... The list goes on.

Brian repeatedly breaks new ground with his vision, ideas, arguments, and experiments. He is a creative thought-leader because he constantly introduces new theories, explanations, viewpoints, and ideas within the marketing and digital worlds. Above all, Brian trusts his gut, is guided by passion, and isn't afraid to stand out with a different, challenging, or contrasting opinion. It's what separates him from the pack.

Challenge the status quo

No matter how much success he has already achieved, Brian remains motivated to keep achieving. What drives him? 'I would love to say it's just the splendour of creating delight and enchantment. You do have to remind yourself that you do have a positive impact and that you do help people with your work', he says. 'Most of the time I'm inspired by the ignorance, or the arrogance, of the state of things or the people whom others follow as their messiahs or their Pied Pipers.'

There are a lot of buzzwords, or buzz concepts, that Brian challenges. 'Certain people have certain charms, a certain mystique or elements of allure that are easy to follow, or believe in, and until they're challenged, they become the standard. So I don't claim to be the most popular person, nor do I try to be. I just really try to show anyone who will listen the possibilities of what happens when you question things; when you question everything.' (See? Yoda.)

Trust your gut

What experiences have led Brian to question everything? I asked him whether he intentionally set out to generate such a major impact with his ideas. 'I'm a design thinker. I have been raised, and most of my professional experience was influenced by, critical thinking: "We can't do this" or "You have to do it this way" or "This is the way it's always been done". And it really made me question, you know, why was it that I was just bumping up against norms or rules? Why was it that I was always having to be told no? Why was it that I was always questioning these things? Was there something wrong with me? It wasn't until recently, until I was comfortable with it, [that] I decided to own the fact [that] I wasn't a rebel. I think I was a dreamer, or an enabler, or someone who just wanted to explore other possibilities because it felt like the right thing to do.'

Brian didn't set out to become a thought-leader. It happened naturally when he followed his instincts. 'The way that I was being pushed down certain parts of protocol didn't feel right. At the end of the day, why do anything that doesn't feel, at your very core, right or comfortable, or inspiring or validating? I wasn't setting out to break things or create new paradigms; I was simply trying to do what felt right. And I continue to do that today.'

The creative force

Brian defines creativity as 'a perspective or an approach that brings to life this idea, or this vision you have, to do something. And that could be in how you walk, it could be a song you write, a piece that you design. Creativity, even the word "innovation", or even the word "artistry" – it's *how* you do something, and the act of doing it is defined by how much you put into it.'

The power of passion

Passion is the driving force behind all of Brian's work: his ideas, his innovations, and his experimentations. 'Without passion, anything you produce just lacks emotion. Not that you need emotion in everything – it just happens to be something that I think is at the heart of what connects with someone else. It's the strings that can talk to the heart, mind, and soul of a person. It's in everything that I do.'

The goals of storytelling

Of all the content that Brian publishes during his travels, the inspirational thoughts and ideas that he jots down on napkins, coasters, and hotel notepads rank among my favourites. They stand out. As someone who understands the value of creating meaningful online experiences, Brian consistently seeks new ways to present his work. 'Your typical analyst template is to write very explicitly and directly what it is that you've found and observed, and what it means. And I've had to train myself to write that way, but this is why I also write books, and create infographics, why I shoot pictures and movies and shows – because I have to explore other elements of creativity.'

Finding different and creative ways to tell stories is as important to him as it is to his audience. 'People hear and see things differently. One story can be told multiple ways. Most of the time we budget time, money, or resources, or all of the above, for one form of communication – for example, a book. But I believe that if you're going to budget for the book, you're also going to have to budget for all of the things that you can do around [it] to communicate what it is you believe, what it is you're impassioned by in other ways.'

When Brian released WTF [What's the Future] of Business?, he joined forces with cartoonist Hugh MacLeod to create artwork and visuals. They were shared across SlideShare, in galleries, infographics, and even on canvas. 'Parts of the book were Instagram-able, or tweet-able, and all of this takes architecture, which takes creativity, which starts with vision, which starts with passion', he explains.

Not letting fear slam on the brakes

As a pioneer of the digital world, Brian's advice for anyone afraid to launch a new product, idea, or concept took me by complete surprise.

'Fear is just a manifestation of other things, like laziness – again, ignorance or arrogance – [the] things that just ... prevent you from doing the things you know you need to do. I'm not saying I'm without fear. I'm well aware that I am just sometimes not going to do something because [I know] what it's going to take to do it.'

Brian often quotes Russian novelist Leo Tolstoy: 'Everyone thinks of changing the world, but no one thinks of changing himself.' The problem, he says, is that by not investing in self-change, 'you're forever going to believe the grass is greener on the other side and you're forever going to chase this idea of a dream, rather than realise it.'

In order to truly realise our dreams, Brian insists we have to accept the fact that we must push the societal limitations and constraints on us. 'That's life', he says.

Creativity is the starting point

In his book *WTF [What's the Future] of Business?*, Brian discusses the importance of the experience brands create for consumers. He believes the most creative point for any concept, idea, or invention comes early on, during the design phase.

'I often talk about the differences between creativity, iteration, innovation, and then, ultimately, disruption. Creativity is the beginning of all that stuff, but it could have an iterative result.'

In the case of Apple, for example, as every update after launch is a process of variation, he says the most creative point for its products is at conception. 'Apple is a creative company – I don't think anybody would argue with that – they're also an innovative company because they've broken ground over the years. But from an experiential standpoint, over the last several years they've really been more of an iterative company, from the iPad to the iPad 2, from the iPhone 3, 4, 5, and 6', he points out.

'The true opportunity for experience is measured by the impact of your creativity because you designed the experience. I call that in [my upcoming] book this idea of the "embrace". As I have your attention, and you have mine, what am I going to with it? And that's where creativity can be unleashed. It's not just in the moment where I get your attention; it's what I do with it that is the next landscape for true innovation.'

His advice to a younger Brian Solis

'I don't have an answer to that, because I wouldn't listen to my older self.'

My takeaway: Brian Solis

Don't just do the status quo – what everybody else is doing. If you think and feel differently, be courageous – stand out by challenging others and sharing your ideas with the world.

We can all make an impact if we follow our hearts and our gut instincts. And in the process, we'll live a more meaningful life.

Be proactive and lead the way when creating change. Realise your dreams by pushing past the limitations and constraints in front of you.

Introducing Randi Zuckerberg

A pioneer for women in tech and a successful, media-savvy entrepreneur, Randi is a creative thought-leader who champions an important tech-life balance philosophy in a very gadget-heavy industry. As a wife and mother of two juggling a busy schedule, Randi devotes time and effort to expressing and exercising her creativity, and in the process ticks huge goals off her 'bucket list'.

After six years as a marketing executive at Facebook, Randi launched her own digital company, Zuckerberg Media, as well as *Dot Complicated*, a lifestyle website that focuses on the challenges associated with achieving tech-life balance. *Dot Complicated's* success for Zuckerberg, its editor-in-chief, opened the door to a two-book deal with HarperCollins. She wrote the nonfiction memoir *Dot Complicated*, which topped *The New York Times* best-seller list, as well as a children's picture book, *Dot*, both of which focus on 'untangling our wired lives'.

Randi delivers sold-out keynotes across the world, has a radio show on Sirius XM, and in 2014 fulfilled a lifelong dream to perform in a New York Broadway show (as Regina from *Rock of Ages*). Most recently, she's been elected to the United Nations Global Entrepreneurs Council and the World Economic Forum's Global Council on Social Media, to name just a few of her many impressive achievements.

Creativity is key

Whether it's social media, Broadway, books, TV, or the speaking world, creativity is a key part of her every endeavour. What exactly does creativity mean to Randi? 'Being different ... being fearless and not being afraid to pursue your own ideas, your own adventures, your own passions, even in the face of everyone else telling you that it's wrong, or you shouldn't. [It's] not being afraid to follow your heart and your passion.'

Randi understands the value of artistic expression at all ages and says she encourages her son to indulge in his own artistic desires (and no doubt she will do the same with her second son, who was born after my interview with her). 'Creativity is one of those things that gets beaten out of you [in our education system] at a young age because it's, like, "Learn this way to do well on tests. Read this way. Do math." Decades down the line, you realise that it's actually something that's celebrated, and you … wish that maybe you'd held onto it from when you were younger. All of the best ideas, companies, and innovations come out of really creative, out-of-the-box thinking. The big companies of tomorrow aren't going to happen by just sitting around doing the same things that we're doing today.'

Passion is paramount

Randi has achieved more once-in-a-lifetime accomplishments than most people, and passion has been her driving force. 'I feel like everyone knows, inside their heart, what they really want to be doing – what really makes them excited and energised to get out of bed in the morning. And if you're not doing that, you're not living your life to your full potential. If you're always, every day, waking up and shoving a piece of your soul – burying it and shoving it away – you're just not accomplishing what you're meant to accomplish on this earth, and there's just no way that you can ever truly be very happy.'

Believing in yourself while pursuing your goals is so important, she says. 'I certainly never, ever thought that I would wind up on Broadway. That was, kind of, the number one thing on my life bucket list. It doesn't matter what age you are, what experience you have – really, any dream can come true if you set your mind and your positive energy and thoughts to it. Everyone around you will tell you, "No, no, no, you can't!" but all you need to do is really believe in yourself and keep marching forward.'

Randi says that, as life changes, our priorities change. As we grow and develop, we need to keep an open mind, and an open heart. 'If you had talked to me five years ago, I would not have been so passionate about family or about unplugging, but because of where

I am in my life now, that's become a new, really important passion area for me. It's also OK if your passions change over time.'

With creativity comes clarity

Expressing her creativity wasn't always her top priority, but after years of working long and hard, Randi discovered how much she needed it. 'When I started off in Silicon Valley, I was just working around the clock, all the time. Investing in myself [was] the last thing on my to-do list every day.' Then she hit a point where she had to change her thinking.

'I realised that not having that creativity and theatre and expression in my life was really holding me back from accomplishing all that I could accomplish. It was really important to me to take a step back and say, "OK, I'm probably not going to be a professional actress, but how can I make creativity and theatre a regular part of my day-to-day life such that it enhances my career?"'

Randi realised that, as she started to invest in herself, she learned a lot about what was important to her, and what she should be focusing on. Giving expression to her creativity became very important. 'At the end of your life, you don't sit there and think, "Oh, I wish I'd worked a little harder, I wish I'd spent more hours at a desk looking at my laptop." What I'm going to think at the end of my life is: "I wish I'd checked that experience off my bucket list, I wish I'd sung on Broadway, or I wish I'd travelled"', she explains. 'I feel like, why wait until you're 50, 60 years old to start checking things off your bucket list? Why not start now? As you start investing in yourself, and trying to check those things off your bucket list, it also teaches you a lot about what's important to you, and what you should be focusing on.'

Taking risks

Randi played a key role in Facebook's early development, including launching *Facebook Live*, a TV-style news show that hosted the likes of President Obama and Katy Perry and scored her an Emmy nomination. After six and a half years, she left Facebook to pursue other career dreams. The decision was a scary one.

'Everyone faces a huge fear when you go out on a limb on your own, whether you're going off to college for the first time or taking a step into that new relationship you're starting. Anything new brings a lot of fear. You wonder, "Are other people going to think this is a good idea, or just me?" You're ... clouded by thoughts of what everyone else is going to think.

'As you get your feet wet, you get comfortable and stop caring so much about what other people think. You start just trying to be the best that you can be. So, it was definitely scary. I had never started a company before but I just felt like the time was really right, and if I didn't do it then, I would probably be procrastinating another five years.'

When it comes to choosing when to make a career change, or take a big risk, Randi admits that there's really no ideal time to do it. 'Everyone says, "There's no great time to have a baby", or "There's no great time to move your house". Similarly, there's no great time to leave a wonderful job and go start your own company. So, I just thought, I'll do this now before I have second thoughts on it because there's never going to be a better time than right now.'

Making mistakes

'I'm a firm believer that you learn a lot more from your mistakes than your successes. And it's only truly a mistake if you make it again.'

Balancing work and life

'You can't do everything well every day. There's no such thing as a superhuman unless ... you have a staff of 30 people following you around at your heels every second, making you perfect. And even then I still don't think you can have it all, every day.

'When I wake up in the morning I think, OK, what are one or two things that I'm going to do really well today? I know I can't do 10 things well today but I can do two things really well today. As long as you're not choosing work every single day of your life, or family every single day of your life, or just going to the gym 12 hours a day, as long as it balances out over the long run, I think that's what it means to have it all – not necessarily that you have to do it all, every day.'

Women in tech

As a strong female figure in the male-dominated tech industry, Randi is convinced that women bring a much-needed voice to the table. 'Women bring a new way of thinking, and a lot of these companies – a large percentage of their user base is women – so they're not serving themselves well if they have a company entirely led by men on the executive team and the product team. We bring a wonderful empathy and a new kind of leadership to the team that can really help companies succeed.'

Randi points out that 90 per cent of today's computer science graduates are men, and the focus of a lot of today's tech products reflects this. 'You see so many products that you're, like, "Oh, that's for young men in their 20s because that's what young men feel comfortable building, that's what men feel comfortable investing in." And it's really difficult to change it. You can feel like you're pushing a boulder up a hill. It's always hard to be the minority in something. It's always hard when you feel like you have to scream louder than everyone else to be heard because everyone else is thinking in [one] way, and you're thinking in [another].'

Her one regret was not having taken more technical courses so that she could speak the language of the Silicon Valley engineers. 'I really encourage young women to take some coding, graphic design, [and] technical courses. I really hope that the women in there continue to fight the good fight, so that it's better for all the next generations to come.'

The perks of unplugging

Committing to switching off is one thing Randi wants to impress upon younger generations. 'I talk a lot about unplugging. Early in my career I felt a lot of pressure to be connected, and answering emails within five minutes of receiving them, and always being reachable online', she says. 'I've realised that it's impossible to be creative and to think "big picture" when you're constantly, like, "What email am I getting? What text am I responding to?" Taking that time to be unreachable and unavailable is often the time when you get your best thinking done', she insists.

Her advice to a younger Randi Zuckerberg

'I really thought when I was younger that there was only one path to get to a dream – like my dream of being on Broadway. I thought the only way to get there was to audition, and have an agent, and stand in casting lines, and that was the way to go. And when I couldn't figure out how to get there, I kind of gave up on it. What I've realised [is that], in life, there are hundreds of ways to get to the end of every dream. Just because one door seems closed to you, go through the fire escape, go through the window, climb up [onto] the roof. Ninety-nine per cent of people are going to go through the front door, and so the people who are really going to be successful are going to [get in] somewhere else.'

My takeaway: Randi Zuckerberg

Having it all doesn't mean ticking all the boxes and living a perfect life. Instead, it's about balancing your priorities in a way that permits you to do the best you can with what matters most to you.

Also, there is never a perfect time to take a creative risk. Right now is as perfect as it gets. So, if you have a dream (especially if it's joining the cast of a Broadway show), find a way to make it happen. You'll have a greater shot at success and standing out if you create a different path to that of everybody else.

Chapter
14

YOUR TURN: ENCOURAGE YOUR OWN CREATIVITY

One of the most challenging parts of the creative process is idea generation. In order to dream up the best ideas, you need to give yourself the best shot at making this happen. And you can generate ideas at any time – I promise. It has nothing to do with your IQ, your upbringing, or even whether or not you finished high school. As many creative aficionados will agree (especially Mark Malkoff; see Chapter 13), creativity is like a muscle. The more you train and exercise it, the stronger it gets.

If you dedicate time to feeding your creativity, developing it, and expanding it, you'll reap the rewards. I'm not promising you'll click your fingers and become the next Picasso or Matt Groening (though, how cool would that be?) but I can guarantee that there are strategies and processes you can put in place on a daily basis to foster, nurture, and encourage your own creative juices. And these strategies will help you push through creative blocks, which are inevitable, no matter who you are. When I'm sitting in front of my computer, I often have moments when my brain freezes. Hello?

Hello?? Nope, nothing. It happened dozens of times while writing this book. (So, if you see any blank pages, you'll know why.)

Thankfully, there are ways around these blocks, tactics we can all use. Don't worry, it's not a painful process. After all, we're not talking about scheduling in calendar time to sort through your taxes and your accounting. *Snoooooze.* This is heaps more fun.

Step 1: Open your imagination

All of the world's best innovations and creations started with one thing: an idea, a hope, a dream. Someone, somewhere, said: 'What if...?' or 'Imagine if I could...?' or 'How cool would it be to...?' From Facebook's conception, to the ground-breaking iPhone, or even the invention of Pringles (potato chips in a cardboard can), they all started with an idea.

Dreaming up ideas is a fundamental part of the creative process. As we grow older, our imagination shuts down. I'm saying 'Open your imagination. Explore ideas. Daydream. And dream big.' And write it all down. For all you know, a note you jot down this afternoon could change your entire future. It could mark the beginning of your own Pringles-in-a-can adventure.

Step 2: Identify your passions

Creativity is fuelled by passion so you want to identify the things you're most passionate about. What topic do you find yourself reading countless articles about? What's an activity you can do for hours on end, without ever getting bored? What's an art form you wish you could create, or a skill you'd love to possess? Identify what fires you up and start there.

You'll find your strongest motivation when you care about what you're working on. I'm not guaranteeing you'll be able to transform your shower rendition of Whitney Houston's 'I Will Always Love You' into a No. 1 iTunes hit, but go ahead and try, by all means. Creativity enriches us and it's good for the soul, so even if you don't get any downloads, you'll still benefit from the process. Or, if you tell me your favourite thing to do is to sit on the couch, drink beer, and watch football, I would say that there are thousands of yet-to-be-invented projects and gadgets in the areas of sport, relaxation, technology, and booze. Whatever your passions are, follow them. We are the most creative when we love what we're doing.

Step 3: Say yes to new experiences

We all get stuck in routines and patterns. It's easy being a creature of habit. I know. I'm guilty of it – big time. The downside of doing the same thing day in and day out is that we're not learning anything new, which gives us limited life experiences to draw upon creatively. As much as I would love to just watch the same TV shows, eat the same foods, and listen to the same music over and over, I understand the value – no, the necessity – of trying new things.

Creative thought-leader Judy Carter is a huge advocate of doing something different and making different choices because those changes are what bring new opportunities. Now, I am in no way advocating that you embark on daredevil activities – trust me, you will never catch me skydiving – but I do make a point of trying new endeavours because you never know who you'll meet, what you'll experience, or how it will make you feel.

So, add something new into your calendar this week (and, no, cleaning out the garage doesn't count). Sign up for a Thai cooking lesson, join your salsa-dancing friend, or agree to model for a life drawing class. Whatever you're into, just say yes. The more life experiences you have to draw from, the greater your pool of creative inspiration will be.

'Life isn't about finding yourself. Life is about creating yourself.'

Playwright and Nobel Prize in Literature winner George Bernard Shaw[88]

Step 4: Schedule downtime

Creativity can rev us up, but it can also demand a lot of brainpower and energy. It's important to recharge as often as you can.

I'm not a meditation guru – I could actually benefit from becoming much more Zen in life – but I understand the importance of switching off. Whether that means watching episode after episode of *Modern Family*, cooking up a storm in your kitchen (for Instagram, obviously) or heading to your favourite coffee shop for your 15th double-shot latte, take a break and have some downtime. Or uptime, if you're that latte drinker. The benefits will be enormous. It will help you replenish your creative energy while re-energising you for the task ahead. You'll likely find that your best creative ideas come to you when you're not focusing on them at all.

Step 5: Indulge in other creative disciplines

You never know where you'll find inspiration – until, of course, you find it.

Exploring the way other people express their creativity can be eye-opening, so if you're thinking about exploring new art forms or there's a skill set you don't have but you wish you did, give it a shot. It's never too late to learn something new.

Do you love music? Try laying your own beats in Garage Band. Do you dream of being on TV? Start making your own YouTube videos. Do you want to write a sitcom? Get in line. I love graphic design, so 10 years ago I taught myself the basics in Photoshop. I may not have become a graphic designer but I've become really good at putting my face on Naomi Campbell's body. It's made dieting so much easier.

'It is never too late to be what you might have been.'

Author and journalist Mary Ann Evans (aka George Eliot)[89]

Step 6: Bounce your ideas off creative confidants

When you decide to share a creative idea with the world, it can often feel like you're sharing a tiny piece of your soul with, well, everybody. Um, that's because you are, to put it bluntly.

Once your idea is actualised and shared, people love it, loathe it, praise it, snob it off, and more. To help you work up the courage to reach your own 'showtime', it helps if you have a creative confidant. If you can find people – or even just one person – who you trust, who respect your ideas and understand your vision, tell them about your creative work before you tell the world. Find someone who is positive and encouraging. Show them the scarf you knitted, send them the poem you penned, ask them to watch your 15-second video before you upload it for the Instaworld to see. This will help in several ways. First, by talking to this person about your idea, by detailing it and fleshing it out, it will help clarify it in your mind. Second, having supportive encouragement and, in the best cases, constructive criticism, can make a good idea better, a great idea brilliant, and, what's more, it can save you from prematurely sharing a sloppy idea with the world.

Bouncing ideas off all of the important people in my life – for my comedy shows, my career changes, the blogs I write, the videos I make, and especially the content and direction of this book – has transformed, enhanced, and improved my work in immeasurable ways.

I should also mention that should the person you choose *not* like your ideas, you can always bribe them with cookies and cakes. It's a tried and tested approach that almost always gets a positive response. At least that's been my experience.

Step 7: Create your own inspiration

To inspire creativity, you have to feel, well, inspired. In order to foster inner creative motivation, surround yourself with things that inspire you, to get motivated from the outside. The best place to start is your workspace, where you spend endless hours answering emails, preparing campaign budgets and chatting on Facebook messenger. Oh, come on, we all do it. Whether you work in a cubicle in a city high-rise or you've set up your laptop behind a pile of laundry in your living room, the space you set up as your workstation should inspire creativity, and, equally as important, productivity.

Look around any work area and you'll see desks decorated with family photos, birthday cards, mementos reflective of a hobby or two, possibly industry accolades – and most definitely some Cup-a-Soup sachets, especially if it's winter. Personalising your workspace is beneficial, so, by all means, keep it up. But in among all of the stuff you already have, add some passion reminders – and by this I mean the things you can't live without: items you love looking at and using, even things you wish you had created yourself.

Choose things that relate directly to your creative work. Surrounding my Mac, for example, I have a Boo mug and a Boo toy (I already told you I want to adopt him as my digital pet), I have Facebook stationery (I'm only a little addicted), I have all of my iPhone boxes because they're clean, white, and perfectly Apple, I have special pens, creative writing journals, and Jerry Seinfeld's and Ellen DeGeneres's autobiographies, because what's life without comedy? Every time I get stuck while writing a presentation, a blog piece, or a joke, I look up at Seinfeld's and Ellen's books and am reminded of the type of success I would love to achieve.

Create a clean workspace with things that inspire you and make you feel good. External passion reminders help trigger your own internal buzz.

'You can't wait for inspiration. You have to go after it with a club.'

Author and social activist Jack London[90]

Step 8: Make time to develop your creativity

People often think creativity is something that just hits in the middle of the night, like a bolt of lightning, or during a spiritual trip to Varanasi. While this can be true, when it's your job to come up with new ideas, you can't just wait for inspiration to hit. When creativity is something you depend on and need to draw from every day, you have to find ways to inspire and encourage it, even when you don't feel like being creative. Trust me, it happens.

In his book *Rewire Your Brain*,[91] Dr John B. Arden says that the more often we generate a particular state of mind, such as positivity, for example, the easier it becomes to return to this mindset, and the greater the likelihood that this mindset will become a personality trait. I believe this can be applied to creativity. The more you fix your conscious thought on creativity – and the more time you spend being creative – the easier it will be to return to this creative state of mind, until being creative becomes part of who you are. So, the more you exercise your creativity muscle, the stronger it gets.

Like so many other things in life, practise is essential. If you want to compete in long jump in the Olympics, you need to put in major track-and-field hours. And if you dream of becoming a surgeon, you'll have to watch A LOT of *Grey's Anatomy*. (Disclaimer: I later discovered you need to study the real *Gray's Anatomy* in order to perform any type of surgery. Apparently knowing the intimate details of Meredith and Derek's relationship history does not qualify you to enter an operating theatre.)

Ultimately, your creative process is a routine. So, invest time into exercising it. Are you a morning person? A night owl? Maybe a couch potato? Either way, pencil in a few times this week when you plan to be creative. The more familiar you become with your own creative process, the more comfortable and natural it will feel, and before you know it, your creativity will start to show up when you ask it to.

OK, have you set up your desk and set time aside to be creative? Great! Here are three strategies to help jumpstart your creativity.

Creativity jumpstart idea No. 1: Start doodling

Contrary to popular belief, all the swirls, swishes, and tiny triangles you got in trouble for drawing in school actually encourage creativity. Doodling is very good for the mind.

In her TED Talk, doodling evangelist Sunni Brown explains there are multiple benefits to doodling, including helping to sharpen our focus. She says we engage at least four learning methods when we doodle. We are reading and drawing, as well as using our mind (visually), our body (kinaesthetically), and our auditory system, because we process information as we doodle.[92]

Feel free to start doodling right now. I have even given you a blank page at the end of the book, just for doodles. Tweet me your doodles! (That doesn't sound right at all … but you know what I mean.)

Sometimes I use my doodles as a vision board. Here's me on a boat with Brad Pitt, sailing away as newlyweds. Don't worry, Angelina is on board too. Somebody had to prepare the cocktails, obviously.

Creativity jumpstart idea No. 2: Act out your ideas

In comedy, an 'act-out' is when you physically act out a joke. It's where you become a character, a person, an object or an animal. Judy Carter talks about this in her book, *The Comedy Bible*.[93] It's funnier for the audience and more fun for you because you *become* the moment.

When your body is still, it can be difficult to conjure up the energy you need to drive new ideas. Getting physical helps inspire creativity by getting you out of your head and into your body. So, get up! Talk out your ideas, animate them, act them out, bring them to life. A word of warning with this one though: make sure you lock your door while doing it!

Creativity jumpstart idea No. 3: Put yourself in someone else's shoes

The best way to find new solutions to old problems is by seeing things from a different perspective. Looking at situations differently encourages a new way of thinking. If you target mostly women with your product, what happens if you try to target men? If your audience consists of mostly the middle-aged, how would you target a teenager? Make time to step into someone else's shoes (preferably Manolo Blahniks) because seeing things differently helps you come up with fresh ideas.

Step 9: Don't critique your ideas

Sometimes our biggest creative enemy is ourselves. That's right. Us. You and me. We can be our biggest supporter or our harshest critic. We all have an inner voice that can barrack for us and help us push through tough situations, or it can feed into our fears and doubts, providing us with every reason in the world as to why we should stop in our tracks and not follow through on a project or idea.

While you're brainstorming, try to turn off your inner critic. Don't listen to your inner lawyer, your inner accountant, your mum's voice, or your partner's voice. As hard as it is to resist, you'll get the most out of a brainstorming session if you push past the 'No, that's not possible', because the unimpeded flow of ideas is an essential part of the creative process. Instead, follow your ideas down your own yellow brick road – just let them run and try to keep up. No matter how crazy they seem, or how unrealistic they become, don't interfere with your imagination mid-journey. In fact, I would actually encourage you to try to push the boundaries of your own creativity. Exaggerate your vision, emphasise your ideas, be outrageous and over the top. The more broadly you cast your brainstorming, the more ideas you'll have to work with when you wrap up your session. And, when you are finally done – when you've reached your own version of Emerald City – then, and only then, apply your wait-can-this-actually-happen filter. And be realistic. Not all ideas will be winners. Some might be ridiculous, even terrifying, while others might be complete gems, and so timely that you can't believe you never thought of them before.

'If at first the idea is not absurd, then there is no hope for it.'

Theoretical physicist Albert Einstein[94]

Step 10: Capture your ideas

Sometimes the best ideas hit us at the most inconvenient times – trekking through the Amazon without a pen and paper, driving in our car on the freeway, or during karaoke sessions in the shower. It's true, we can't always control when creative ideas hit, but with practice we can become more creative more of the time, which means we can be more prepared for our own creativity. No matter what you're working on, always capture your ideas. Record them in a voice memo, email them to yourself, or write them on a restaurant napkin using a stranger's eyeliner – just get them out. This will make space for new ideas to come in and, as you collect lists of ideas, you'll gain more confidence in your own creativity.

And always – *always* – keep a list of your ideas: the good, the bad, and even the downright cringeworthy. Keep the ones you say yes to, and especially the ones you say no to, because you never know when they'll come in handy.

 ## Don't forget

- Creativity is like a muscle. The more you train it and exercise it, the stronger it gets. So, put on your sweats and sneakers and get to work!

- Set aside time on your calendar to practise being creative.

- Open your imagination. Dream big.

- Identify your passions and pursue them. Start now.

- Create your own inspiration. Fill your workspace with things that inspire you. Feel free to start with this book.

- Start doodling. Unleash your inner da Vinci.

- Test your ideas by acting them out first.

- See the world through someone else's eyes.

- Slot something new and exciting to do on your calendar this week to shake up your life and your creativity.

- Schedule in downtime, just as you schedule in coffees, work meetings, and episodes of *Extreme Makeover*.

- Turn off your inner critic, or at least mute it.

- Try your hand at a new creative discipline.

- Bounce your ideas off someone you trust.

- Capture your ideas by writing them down. Yes, all of them.

- Put your ideas into action. Pick a goal for this week, create a to-do list with a timeline, and get it done. Go!

GLOSSARY:
A TWISTING OF TERMS

Most content marketing and social media books provide you with a straightforward glossary of terms with widely accepted definitions. Because this book is focused on creativity, I have instead chosen to take a different approach and have you step into my shoes to see what these phrases and words mean to me.

(For official definitions of the terms below, any search engine should do.)

ALGORITHM
The process of acquiring statistical data and analysis that allows online marketing and social media 'gurus' to exorbitantly overcharge customers.

ANDROID
As an iPhone addict, I haven't a clue how to define or describe Android phones. They're beneath me.

APP
Allows any of us to become experts in seconds and, often, completely for free. If you're willing, apps can totally run (and rule) your life. I recently downloaded an app for breathing. I'm still here, so I can safely say it was totally worth the $1.99 price tag.

AVATAR
Turning nerds into superheroes on social media profiles.

BIO

A description on your social profile briefly describing who you wish you were and the values you think people would like you to have.

BLOCK

It's like an online restraining order for Twitter, only immediately effective. It's great to protect yourself against any negativity from trolls, but terrible when you bump into that person you've been blocking for the past 12 months ... at your family reunion.

BLOG

A modern-day version of a 'Dear Diary' entry. Responsible for turning millions of stay-at-home mums into authors – myself included (minus the kid part).

BLOGGER

Someone who sits at their computer writing about something they're passionate about, while wearing pyjama pants and eating last night's leftover pizza. I once found a blog about becoming a better sleepwalker. Clearly, passion areas are subjective.

BLOGOSPHERE/TWITTERSPHERE

A nerdy and annoying made-up word used to describe the ethers that encompass both the blog and Twitter worlds. Please don't ever let me hear you use the 'sphere' phrases.

BRAND ADVOCATE

The people to whom you should be sending all of your sales, marketing, and promo budgets.

BUZZFEED

The creator of some of the internet's most vital quizzes, including 'Which Disney Princess Are You?' and 'Which "Buffy The Vampire Slayer" character are you?' Caution: be careful what you click on. I have lost hours of my life to these games.

CANDY CRUSH

A Facebook game that encourages addicted players to foster addiction within their friendship groups by offering bonus points for new recruits. An invitation in my notifications for Candy Crush turns a current Facebook friend into a former Facebook friend. See also *Unfriending*.

CIRCLES

In Google Plus, circles allow you to group your friends and connections together. Don't worry, I don't know how to use them either. Used predominantly by Google employees, circles weren't set up for the common people.

CLICKBAIT

A desperate attempt by editorial publications to lure you to click on a link that will ultimately increase their online traffic. Clickbait almost always leads to great disappointment for audiences. It's pretty much like every single online dating profile I've ever seen.

CLICK-THROUGH RATE

Measures the amount of people who fell for the clickbait. Each click represents heartbreak and disillusionment.

CLOUD

The thing that nobody can successfully explain to anybody else. Here's my attempt: A modern-day solution to a floppy disc that exists somewhere between the planet Pluto and your Apple ID. It safely stores all of your personal and private photos, documents, and videos … unless you're a celebrity, that is.

COMMENT

Where the world's shortest sentence can take hours of pre-post deliberation.

COMMUNITY MANAGEMENT
An underestimated and often undervalued time-intensive job that demands the person serving in the role to act as therapist, lawyer, councillor, law enforcer, judge, medium, translator, relationship expert, and occasional politician.

CONNECTION (LINKEDIN)
A person who you may either have met once, want to meet, or will never, ever meet. No matter the source of your relationship, your connection to them helps boost your LinkedIn numbers so everybody wins. If you and I aren't yet connected, hit me up. Win-win.

COVER PHOTO
The image used at the top of your personal social media profile or brand page to convey the vibe of a world you wish you were immersed in. Most commonly sunsets, silhouettes, and the Northern Lights.

CRAIGSLIST
U.S.-based website where people sell, trade, and offer just about everything. Last time I was on Craigslist, I found a guy auctioning stomach lint to the highest bidder. Gross.

CRISIS MANAGEMENT
When you've done something wrong online and somebody has a screen shot of it; always involves some kind of damage repair. My advice: remorse and repentance. Say you're sorry.

CROWDFUNDING
A very public way to ask people to back your passion project through the donation of funds in exchange for online rewards and attention. In 2014, a guy in the States raised more than $55,000 to make a potato salad on Kickstarter.[95] It seems dreams really do come true.

DIRECT MESSAGE

Messaging someone privately on Twitter. You can only message users who follow you and vice versa. Lady Gaga follows me (and 132,000 other people). I have sent her 25 DMs and she hasn't responded yet. I'm sure she's just busy crafting the perfect reply (see also *Comment*). I'll continue to be patient … and persistent.

DISPLAY AD

The Holy Grail for digital sales and marketing teams. The only time they're clicked on is by accident.

DUCK FACES

If selfies weren't bad enough, people make duck faces in photos to look 'sexy'. Since when did ducks become sexy? Pick another animal, please.

EBOOK

An electronic, downloadable version of a book that is slowly putting book stores out of business. I don't know about you but I've never successfully read an entire eBook. Mine are safely tucked away in my Kindle library, collecting cyber dust. Oh, by the way, of course this book is available as an eBook. Are you reading this on your iPad? And you've made it this far??

EMOJI

Allowing those of us who have always been held back by emotional issues to finally, fully express ourselves in SMS using tiny Japanese icons.

ENGAGEMENT

The act of communicating with your online network. Premium relationship skills are required, without having to splash thousands on a diamond-carat investment. Typically easier to engage with people online than the person you share your bed with at night.

EYE CONTACT
Something we never do. See also *Face to Face.*

FACE TO FACE
A form of communication used until the late '90s that involved two people connecting, in person, with eye contact. Face to face has been null and void since the release of the Nokia 3210 in 1999.

FACEBOOK
Promoting chronic oversharing and endless procrastination, Facebook has been the number one source for remembering birthdays since its launch over a decade ago.

FACEBOOK FANS
The people who Like your Facebook page. With hundreds of online companies offering free Likes for cash, Facebook fans are not a true measure of a brand's success. See first whether they speak the same language to determine whether they even understand what you're posting.

FACEBOOK GROUP
Because we don't have enough ways to communicate already.

FACETIME
The button you accidentally push when you want to make a phone call when you aren't concentrating. Also, the iPhone function that makes you shockingly aware of how horrible you look without any make-up.

FAVOURITE
A form of praise and acknowledgement you can give another user on Twitter. Ranks below a Facebook Like but above a gold star in kindergarten.

FILTER

Can make us look prettier, skinnier, healthier, more tanned, more cultured, and richer. Rivals popular make-up brands in its ability to cover up zits, blemishes, and hangovers.

FOLLOWER

Something we are terrified of in real life but wish we had more of online.

FOMO

'Fear of missing out'; a condition that affects mostly teenagers, One Direction fans, and single females aged 33 and over. (At the time of this book's release I was 33.)

FORUMS

A place where people go to bond, complain to each other, and get horrible, worst-case-scenario medical advice from unqualified patients suffering similar symptoms halfway across the world. Where hypochondriacs flourish.

FOURSQUARE

A once popular location check-in app. Remember when everyone wanted to be the mayor of McDonald's? Yeah, not anymore.

FRIENDS

Your friends online are not the same as they are in real life. You tag them in photos, you're jealous of their food pictures, and you desperately hope they saw that one great shot of you at the Four Seasons hotel swimming pool wearing your brand new bikini (or is that just me?). Chances are you haven't actually seen or spoken to 95 per cent of your online friends since 1994. The other five per cent you haven't actually met. Ah, online life.

GIF

If we're going for the technical explanation, it's a graphic interchange format that allows single images … blah, blah, blah, something 8-bit. Basically, the key point here is: do we pronounce it 'gif' or 'jif'? I still don't know.

GOOGLE

Owns almost all of the internet, including YouTube, Blogger, Google Drive, Google Plus, Nexus, and Chrome. Answers all of life's biggest questions, such as 'Why is my eye twitching?' Google knows your likes and dislikes and the secret websites you won't ever admit to visiting, as well as all of the medical symptoms you've presented with over the past 12 months. Or maybe that's just me. Point being, Google basically owns you too.

GOOGLING

Things you do to clothes before buying them, employees before hiring them, and men before dating them.

HASHTAG

One of the most commonly misused internet trends. Too many social media users are under the false impression that these make everything sound cooler. Hashtags need strict laws and rules, and especially character limits to #prevententiresentencesfrombeinghashtagged. Also, please refrain from using hashtags in everyday conversation.

HOOTSUITE

A social media management tool that allows you to schedule posts, engage with your audience, and gather analytics across multiple social media platforms, all while watching episodes of *Entourage*. Perfect for those who are too busy being social in real life to be social in real-time online. At least, that's what I've heard.

HTML

HTML is the language – the code – used to write and create internet pages. If you want to land a date with one of today's hottest web geeks, I recommend you learn to speak their language. <format>Immediately.com/</format>

INFLUENCER

The name given to anyone with great online reach. With a massive Twitter account, heaps of Facebook fans, and loads of LinkedIn connections, they're the online version of the popular kids at school. Ironically, though, they were probably the biggest nerds at school.

INFOGRAPHIC

Presenting complex data and statistics in the form of pretty pictures and simple graphics because we all have short attention … uh, what?

INSTAGRAM

Responsible for the popularity of selfies, filters, online egos, and hashtags, it's a visually driven social network where people showcase the things that matter to them, and the things they believe matter to others. Instagram is fuelled by pictures of feet in the sand, pug puppies, and Kim Kardashian's iPhone collection.

INSTANT MESSAGING

The modern-day version of passing notes in class, private messaging is the perfect way to organise a dinner with friends or avoid the harsh awkwardness of breaking up with someone in person. See also *Face to Face*.

iPHONE

Something you can't function without. In many cases, iPhones are more meaningful than friends, family, and your long-term partner.

KEYWORDS

Commonly used search terms you wish people would associate with you. 'Wish' being the, well, key word.

LIKE

An online indication used to evaluate one's worth on Facebook, Instagram, LinkedIn and Pinterest. Be cautious and watch your mouse on Facebook. One accidental graze of the Like button will immediately reveal that you're not actually the fun, detached former partner you so desperately want your ex to believe you are.

LINKEDIN

A social network for the corporate world. Great for digging up strangers' work histories, connecting with people you've never met, and being reminded to congratulate a random connection from your past on their recent promotion.

LINKEDIN ENDORSEMENT

Most users share a common goal of attracting as many endorsements as humanly, physically possible. Please note: endorsements cannot be taken seriously. Last week He-Man endorsed me as Master of the Universe. Twice.

LOL

Used to denote laugh out loud, an action that none of us ever *actually* do when we use it. Despite being hideously overused, LOL is an acronym that has magically managed to remain relevant and popular. No idea how.

MASHABLE

One of the world's leading social media, tech, and digital news platforms. It's one of the major sources of all the content I share on Facebook and Twitter that makes me look tech-savvy and on the cutting edge of everything that's cool online.

MEETUP
An offline meet-up group for online junkies. An excellent way to shatter the fantasy of who Meetup members envision their new online friends to be. In other words, destroying online dreams, one nature meet-up hike at a time.

MEME
One of the most annoying *and* entertaining online content concepts ever created that spreads faster than bird flu. Famous memes include the dramatic chipmunk, LOLcats, and my personal favourite, Grumpy Cat. To all the mums and dads out there: it's pronounced meem. Not me-me. OK?

MESSENGER
The day Mark Zuckerberg invented timestamps showing when we viewed messages from our friends was the day we all started pretending to stop logging into Messenger.

MYSPACE
The original and ... not the best. The place where it all began for social networks and a place we will never return to. If you still have a MySpace page, you should probably put this book down right now. Unless you're Justin Timberlake, in which case, please tweet me at @JordanaOZ.

NEWS FEED
The source for all your daily procrastination thrown together by your Facebook friends and the brands you follow. A never-ending stream of news, gossip, sonogram pics, relationship breakup updates, political arguments, and targeted ads that directly relate to the last internet search you did while accidentally leaving your Facebook browser tab open. Creepy.

ONLINE STALKING
The act of keeping tabs on your ex-partners, most often without their knowledge or consent. Can involve spending hours looking through their Facebook photo albums, reading their personal comments, and saving their family photos to your desktop to make a collage. Oh ... just me?

OVERSHARING
The act of sharing too much information across your social media accounts. We all have friends who think we need to see 12 photos a day of their ginger cat because, you know, 11 is simply not enough.

PINTEREST
A visual representation of the life you'll never have. It's a place to showcase your favourite collection of Martha Stewart-esque DIY lifestyle images for your home, office, kitchen, and wardrobe. Disclaimer: Pinterest boards and collections are only attainable if you have all the time in the world and if money grows on trees.

PODCAST
The friend that you don't set time aside for, but one who you can't live without when it comes to doing the dishes, laundry, long drives, or those 20 lame minutes on the treadmill.

REDDIT
A powerful content-sharing platform boasting the most uninviting user interface on the whole web. Responsible for making heaps of content go viral, including the original Grumpy Cat image.

RETWEET
An authentic or forced public endorsement of someone else's idea, image, or thought. RTs are a great way to appear present and engaged on Twitter without much effort at all.

SCREEN SHOT

Destroying lives, capturing mistakes, and keeping people accountable since the iPhone 3 first came out in 2009.

SEARCH ENGINE OPTIMISATION (SEO)

A means of perfecting and presenting your online content so that you come up at the top of search results. Basically, the same rules apply offline as online: Look hot, popular, and carry a small Chihuahua in your purse so that people will notice you. Caution: If an SEO company guarantees they have the perfect formula to keep you at the No. 1 position on searches forever, they're lying. You've been warned.

SELFIE STICK

The thing that would totally improve your photo collection – but that you never want to be caught using in public.

SELFIES

My tips:

1. No wrinkles, no mirror, no arm in the shot
2. Snap at a flattering 30-degree angle
3. Choose an Instagram filter that perfectly suits your complexion

SIRI

Full of attitude, Siri has an answer for everything. Master at avoiding confrontation, when I asked Siri if I looked fat, she said, 'I can't see you.' Well-played, Apple. Men could learn a lot from Siri.

SKYPE

Has turned business meetings in your underwear from a dream into a reality.

SLIDESHARE

Finally! A place to parade that PowerPoint presentation you stayed up all night perfecting. Now, everyone gets to see your superior master slide, duplicate slide, text box, and pie chart skills.

SMARTPHONE

Makes avoiding human contact while still connecting with the world entirely possible from any location that has strong cell reception. Contributes to emotional issues, troubled relationships, and flawed posture.

SMS

Gr8 way 2 spk.

SNAPCHAT

Promoting promiscuity 10 seconds at a time, Snapchat is a popular social network among teens. Most messages last up to 10 seconds before self-imploding. Blink and you'll miss it, but don't be fooled: 'disappearing' never actually means disappearing online.

SOCIAL MEDIA GLOSSARY

Um, *this?*

SOCIAL MEDIA GURUS

The term used by self-confessed social media experts. A word for you gurus: just because you tweet and use Facebook, it doesn't make you the Buddha of social media. Unless your name is Mark Zuckerberg.

SOCIAL MEDIA ROI

The illusive, immeasurable statistics keeping social media marketing companies in business.

SPAM

The emails we get from strangers concerned with the quality of our sex lives, or who are distant relatives in Uganda thoughtfully letting us know we've just won $17 million in the latest lottery. Quick, don't miss out!

STATUS UPDATE
Used to whinge, complain, and brag to Facebook friends who haven't yet hidden your posts. Be cautious.

TABLETS
Making our anti-social habits more mobile than ever.

THROWBACK THURSDAY (#TBT)
A hideous excuse for people to dig out old baby photos and pictures of a much skinnier, longer-haired version of themselves that nobody wants to see, only to parade them all over Twitter and Instagram. Every. Single. Thursday.

TIMELINE
Your Facebook outline of the key moments and major dates in your life, including when you were born, when you left your last job, and when you had your last mental breakdown.

TINDER
Swipe right for yes; swipe left for no. A beautiful testament to the kind, caring, and compassionate nature of young lovers these days.

TROLL
The scourge of the online world. Anonymous, nasty, and gutless, they're the type of people who stick gum underneath the seats in movie cinemas. You're well within your rights to imagine them with hunchbacks.

TUMBLR
I don't understand it, I don't like it, I find it messy and annoying. It moves too quickly for me and I can't keep up. (Clearly I'm getting too old for this.)

TWEETUP
A real-life meet-up for the online friends with whom you've shared your life in 140 characters or less. It's where you put faces to the ... hashtags.

TWITTER
A great place to stalk celebrities and launch political movements. Decreasing attention spans since 2006.

UNFOLLOW
The ultimate act of Twitter or Instagram rejection. It's like breaking up online.

UNFRIENDING
The cruel act of removing someone from your friends list on Facebook because you can't bear to look at one more status update about how brilliant their Jamaican honeymoon is. So, you punish them by no longer allowing them to see your updates, including yesterday's poached eggs and your latest check-in at Starbucks. Unfriending on Facebook can have real-life consequences. See also *Blocking*.

VINE
A product of Twitter, Vine is a micro-video sharing platform with a six-second video limit. It encourages creative storytelling, short attention spans, and makes Instagram's 15-second videos feel like extended-length documentaries.

VIRAL
Something nobody wants to catch in disease form, but a highly sought-after quality in online content.

WEBINAR
Half an hour of your life you'll never get back.

WHATSAPP

The new family meeting place. Yet another one of Facebook's many investments into our private and personal conversations.

WI-FI

What every coffee shop needs in order to get customers through the front door.

WIKIPEDIA

Replacing the need for librarians and books for more than two decades. Often incredibly factually inaccurate. Updated by egotistical publicists and members of the public. OK, off to update my page!

YELP

Where reviews by nobodies continue to destroy profits and earnings.

YOUTUBE

A video-sharing platform responsible for launching the careers of both talented and untalented humans and animals, such as cats playing pianos, Justin Bieber, and Rebecca Black.

THANK YOU

Hooray! You made it to the end of my book … Or maybe you just skipped straight to the end and haven't actually read any of the chapters. Either way, thanks for being here. I know your time is valuable, and I feel honoured to have captured your attention.

I hope you learned a lot, LOL'd a lot and that you have everything you need to start getting creative with your online content right now. Hopefully the exercises, techniques, tips, lessons, stories, and strategies have inspired you to develop a long parchment-length list of creative ideas. If not, a short Post-it note list is great too, as long as you have what you need to generate and create. Immediately.

Whether it's for work or play, invest in your creativity. It's good for your mind, body, and soul. Find the courage to express your individuality because your uniqueness will make your ideas stand out.

We are all capable of dreaming up ideas, finding the passion and courage to take an idea off our to-do list to turn it into a reality, and, of course, injecting our own unique spin into it to make it truly unforgettable. So, use the strategies I discussed in this book and remember the four ingredients that you already have: imagination, passion, character, and courage. And don't be afraid to be different.

When you create your first meme, video, blog, how-to guide, or even singing goat video that's driven by an idea helped along by this book, I want to know about it. So, please tweet me at @JordanaOZ and use the hashtag #capturemyattention. You can also Instagram me, Facebook me, Vine me, reVine me, retweet me… Just don't Snapchat me. Because, you know...

And we're done!

Well? What are you waiting for? Go on! Start creating!

'One day you will wake up and there won't be any more time to do the things you've always wanted. Do it now.'

Author and lyricist Paulo Coehlo[96]

DOODLING PAGE

ACKNOWLEDGEMENTS

Capture My Attention is far from a solo effort. In fact, I couldn't have written this book without the help and support of a lot of important people. Some special people helped with creative brainstorms, edits, and interviews, while other special people helped by providing moral support, answering endless questions, inspiring my creativity, telling me I was being too much of a perfectionist, or just joining me for a glass of Champagne when I really needed it. These people generously gave up their time and shared their ideas in order to help me move forward in my creative journey and through my career. So here are my thank yous. Family first, then in alphabetical order...

Mum and Dad – Thank you for always believing in me, and for supporting and encouraging my dreams. You are the absolute best and I couldn't do what I do without you. From vet science to journalism, to photography, to radio, to comedy, to speaking, to writing a book, and to whatever else lies ahead, I am so lucky to have your amazing, unconditional support. On that note, thanks also for putting up with me for 33 years – what an achievement!

Noah Borensztajn – Wise, wise Noah. Thanks for possessing all of the wonderful qualities that skipped right past me. I'm so grateful for your amazing advice, insight and support, and your honest feedback on this book (and everything else). Thanks for always making time to balance me when I freak out. You're a (very brave) lifesaver!

Sera Bozza – I admire your creative vision. Thanks for your many brilliant ideas over the years: for your amazing artistic input, for your fashion tips, for always adding a special touch to my comedy material, and for supporting all of my shows by seeing them each three times. Or was it four?

Leah Bonnema – Princess Leah, my fellow creative, fellow comic, and fellow hand sanitiser enthusiast. Thanks for your creative support. I heart our vault.

Fay Burstin – Thanks for inviting me to write all those health stories in my earliest days at the *Herald Sun*, and for your fab support of my comedy. You've been a wonderful mother hen.

John Button – Thanks for always answering 1000 questions with a smile. There's no way I could have made it through the writing process without the help of my favourite pharmacist.

Ness and Andy Chrapot – Thanks for being the perfect practice crowd for my comedy shows. I know that when I see tears, I'm onto something special.

Coffee – You are my everything. You are the first thing I think about in the morning, the last thing I think about at night, and my reason for living. Well, one of them anyway.

Adam Cubito – Thanks to your wicked imagination, I'm able to take my crazy ideas to wonderful new heights. I love your ideas, our creative brainstorms, and our late-night SMS conversations. I dream of a future filled with your green ticks.

Steve Ellen – Thanks for teaching me that having a little bit of every condition actually makes you more balanced and adjusted overall, than not having *anything* of *anything*. Phew! I loved your advice about getting a good sleep the night before the night before, and I appreciate your rearranging your living room to make it look like the perfect studio backdrop.

Facebook – Thank you for helping me procrastinate while writing this book. Without you, this book would probably be twice as long.

Antonella Fedele – Anty, thanks for opening my eyes to so many truths over the years. Your insight astounds me. Thanks for believing in me, encouraging me, always giving me the best advice, and for sending review notes for this book from the most unlikely of places.

Forever friends – To my girls from school who've supported every comedy show, every adventure I've embarked on, and every different incarnation of Jordana over the years, thank you.

Sacha French – From Nova to comedy, to social media, to speaking, thanks for your genuine and wholehearted support every step of the way. It means a lot.

Siobhan Gallagher – Thanks for answering all my questions (*all* my questions), for your honest and entertaining editing feedback, and for revealing your Facebook secrets. It was lots of fun!

Shannon Gettins – One million thank yous for helping me edit my baby (and for all the therapy along the way). I love our LOLs, our doodles, your advice, and, importantly, the ground-breaking realisation that knitting isn't *actually* an asset. I couldn't have done this without you, Shan. Single red shoe forever!

Sarah Grynberg – Darly Darl. Thanks for listening – to everything, all of the time – and being an ear through my entire book-writing journey (and life in general). So lucky!

Hughesy & Kate (Dave Hughes and Kate Langbroek) – Thank you for 12+ years of morning laughs. Between 2001 and 2013, you and coffee (see above) were the only reasons I got out of bed before the sun came up. Your unique brand of comedy helped influence and shape my sense of humour, and working with you at Nova was a dream come true.

Instagram – Thank you for luring me away from Facebook for hours at a time with your nostalgic and romantic-filtered pictures.

Adam Krongold – You were the first person I messaged when I departed Facebook's headquarters as a heartbroken thumb. Thanks for always making me laugh during a crisis.

Kate Langbroek – Katie, what would this book be called if I hadn't bumped into you in the supermarket? Thanks for your hilariously honest feedback. So, do you like my new title?

Naomi Lawson and Jacqui Rosshandler – Jac and Yellow, thanks for always making the effort to come and support my comedy shows in my home away from home, New York City. It's always awesome hearing your laughs among a crowd full of strangers.

LinkedIn – Thanks for creating a social network that masks as work.

David Longfield – By the time you read this thank you note, it means my book is out and my phone calls, therefore, have ended. Thank you for holding my hand through this publishing journey and for your wonderful help, guidance, support, and patience. Did I mention patience, patience, and patience?

Nicole Matejic – Majestic, thanks for your unwavering support of my social media comedy, for giving me advice on the book-writing process, and for that generous introduction way back when.

Kevin McQuillan – Once upon a time you were my university lecturer. Now, you're bringing me into university to *give* lectures. Thanks for opening new doors, and for all your fab support.

Steve Moar – Thanks for listening to all of my complaints, concerns, and crazy ideas over the years (to be fair, you don't really have a choice when I'm lying on your massage table). Thanks also for always helping me when my body freaks out. (Or is that me freaking out?)

Shannon Mullen – Thanks for being an A+ partner-in-crime in Dallas. You played a huge role in helping me capture my *Zucker Up!* videos and I'll always be grateful.

Sharmila Nahna – Thanks for taking a punt on a 'wild card'. It's been an awesome hashtag-filled ride so far! From WC. #youarethebest

Debra and Michael Olenski – Thank you for always going out of your way to introduce me to the right person, at the right place, at the right time. You guys rock.

Panda – Thanks for believing in me, for the endless support and encouragement you've shown over the years, and for your advice, insight, and ideas. Where, oh where, would I be without it?

Pinterest – Thanks for allowing me to instantaneously build a dream wardrobe *and* dream sneaker collection without using any precious cupboard space at all.

Michelle Read – Thanks for helping me brainstorm and talk through some gems over the years. Pucker up!

Ian Royall – Boss! From journalism through to stand-up comedy, your wholehearted support always means a lot to me. Thanks for pulling out your red pen (and emoji keyboard) for this book. Cheers to Toowoomba! (Or is that Innisfail?)

Hayley Rynderman – Lassie! Thanks for suggesting I try photography forever ago. Look where that wonderful journey took me. Genius …

Mona Sherif – Thanks for helping me overcome my addiction to Googling medical conditions, Dr Awesome; it totally freed me up to write this book! Thanks also for your valuable creative input and especially for the LOLs. They're just what the doctor ordered.

Patrick Slevin – Thanks for helping make my music dreams come true by letting me interview and photograph my favourite bands and gigs in the tri-state area. Thanks also for introducing me to the finest NYC establishments – nothing beats used cowboy boots dangling from bar ceilings. Classy.

Zara Swindels-Gross – You told me to write a book, Zara, so… ta dah! Thank you for this golden nugget of advice. I really appreciate it. Tell me, what's next on my to-do list?

Peter Thurin – Thank you for your advice and help early on in my speaking career. I appreciate it.

Twitter – Thanks for always being there. I only hope I can give you back just a tiny hashtag's worth of the joy you've provided me over the years. #sospecial

Carson White – Thanks for always making time to share the best advice and career tips with me. I am really grateful for your help, support, and ideas.

To my creative thought-leaders – I thank you all for your valuable time, honesty, and insight. I have learnt a lot from you.

Judy Carter – My first comedy coach. Thank you for teaching me the comedy ropes, for arranging my debut LA stage spot, and for inspiring me to follow my dream of becoming a speaker. You have so many wonderful lessons to share with the world; you truly are one in a million. *The Comedy Bible* is still the only bible I have ever read from start to finish. Amen.

Mark Malkoff – Thanks for showing me that there is absolutely no limit to our imagination and what we can achieve. Thanks for inspiring me to think crazier, think bigger, and for teaching me one very important lesson: that you don't actually have to ride NYC's dirty subway – you can just ask strangers to carry you uptown.

Cameron Parker – Thanks for being such a great example of how to truly succeed in this ever-changing online world. Your examples of storytelling and nurturing online communities have given me, and my readers, so much to aim for.

Joe Pulizzi – Thanks for your honesty about what it really takes to become a successful entrepreneur – your advice has been incredibly valuable. Thanks also for believing in me and for giving me the opportunity to speak at CMWorld Sydney and at CMWorld Ohio. What an absolute privilege! Both events have always been at the top of my wish list.

Brian Solis – Thanks for showing us all the value of speaking your mind, sticking to your gut, and not being afraid to challenge everything around you. Thanks also for your wonderful support of my social media comedy. When I come to SXSW in my giant Like costume, you're the first person I am having a photo with!

Randi Zuckerberg – Thank you for being an inspiring female figure in the digital world. We need more of you! Thank you also for giving me the opportunity to write for *Dot Complicated*. I love the synchronicity that exists between the philosophy of both your book and your website and the message of my social media comedy.

To all of YOU – Thank you to everyone who has supported the many different facets of my career: my comedy festival shows, my speaking career, my *Zucker Up!* quest, my creative content workshops, my journalism journey, my performances overseas, my passion for all things social media-related, and of course, this book. From the bottom of my heart, THANK YOU.

NOTES

[1] Seth Godin, BrainyQuote.com, http://www.brainyquote.com/quotes/quotes/s/sethgodin541626.html, permission via e-mail February 4, 2015.

[2] Maya Angelou, Goodreads.com, http://www.goodreads.com/quotes/153929-you-can-t-use-up-creativity-the-more-you-use-the.

[3] Mark W. Schaefer, *Social Media Explained: Untangling the world's most misunderstood business trend*, Mark W. Schaefer, 2014, p.12.

[4] Brian Solis, *WTF [What's the Future] of Business: Changing the way businesses create experiences*, John Wiley & Sons, New Jersey, 2013, p.28.

[5] 'What Is Content Marketing?', Content Marketing Institute, http://contentmarketinginstitute.com/what-is-content-marketing.

[6] Brian Solis, permission via e-mail December 18, 2014.

[7] George Beahm, ed, *I, Steve: Steve Jobs in his own words,* Hardie Grant Books, Australia/UK, Kindle edition, 2011, p.31. Quote from the Apple Worldwide Developers Conference, San Jose Convention Center, California, May 13–16, 1997.

[8] Sandra Blakeslee, 'Complex and Hidden Brain in Gut Makes Stomachaches and Butterflies', *New York Times*, January 23, 1996, http://www.nytimes.com/1996/01/23/science/complex-and-hidden-brain-in-gut-makes-stomachaches-and-butterflies.html.

[9] Ellen DeGeneres selfie, 'If only Bradley's arm was longer. Best photo ever. #oscars', Twitter, March 3, 2014, http://twitter.com/theellenshow/status/440322224407314432.

[10] Lisa Baertlein, 'Ellen's Oscar "selfie" crashes Twitter, breaks record', Reuters.com, March 3, 2014, http://www.reuters.com/article/2014/03/03/us-oscars-selfie-idUSBREA220C320140303.

[11] Dove United States, 'Dove Real Beauty Sketches | You're more beautiful than you think', YouTube video, 3:00, doveunitedstates, April 14, 2013, http://www.youtube.com/watch?v=XpaOjMXyJGk.

[12] See Jason Keath, 'The Top 11 Branded Viral Videos of 2013', socialfresh.com, January 8, 2014, http://www.socialfresh.com/top-branded-viral-videos-2013; see also Laura Stampler, 'How Dove's "Real Beauty Sketches" Became the Most Viral Video Ad of All Time', BusinessInsider.com.au, May 23, 2013, http://www.businessinsider.com.au/how-doves-

real-beauty-sketches-became-the-most-viral-ad-video-of-all-time-2013-5; see also Emma Gray, 'Dove's "Real Beauty Sketches" Ad Campaign Tells Women "You're More Beautiful Than You Think"', *The Huffington Post*, April 17, 2013, http://www.huffingtonpost.com/2013/04/15/doves-real-beauty-sketches-ad-campaign-video_n_3088071.html.

[13] Walt Disney, BrainyQuote.com, http://www.brainyquote.com/quotes/quotes/w/waltdisney130027.html.

[14] Steven Spielberg, BrainyQuote.com, http://www.brainyquote.com/quotes/quotes/s/stevenspie113970.html.

[15] J.K. Rowling, BrainyQuote.com, http://www.brainyquote.com/quotes/quotes/j/jkrowlin415661.html.

[16] Oscar Wilde, Goodreads.com, http://www.goodreads.com/quotes/19884-be-yourself-everyone-else-is-already-taken.

[17] Michael Jordan, BrainyQuote.com, http://www.brainyquote.com/quotes/quotes/m/michaeljor167382.html.

[18] Mae West, Goodreads.com, http://www.goodreads.com/quotes/1598-you-only-live-once-but-if-you-do-it-right.

[19] Ellen DeGeneres, 'Ellen at Tulane Commencement 2009', YouTube video, 17:54, Tulane University, March 4, 2010, http://www.youtube.com/watch?v=0e8ToRVOtRo.

[20] *Forbes*, 'The World's Highest-Paid Celebrities – 2015 ranking: #12 Ellen DeGeneres', Forbes.com, http://www.forbes.com/profile/ellen-degeneres.

[21] Lady Gaga, Goodreads.com, http://www.goodreads.com/author/quotes/2945649.Lady_Gaga.

[22] Steve Jobs, 'Steve Jobs' 2005 Stanford Commencement Address', YouTube video, 15:04, Stanford, March 7, 2008 (filmed June 12, 2005), http://www.youtube.com/watch?v=UF8uR6Z6KLc. See also 'Steve Jobs' 2005 Stanford Commencement Address', Stanford News, June 14, 2005, http://news.stanford.edu/news/2005/june15/videos/987.html.

[23] Harriet Cummings, 'Finding Your Brand's Voice: How to shape a tone of voice', Distilled, http://www.distilled.net/tone-of-voice.

[24] Julie Wildhaber, 'Understanding Voice and Tone in Writing: Choosing words to connect with your audience', Grammar Girl – quickanddirtytips.com, July 1, 2010, http://www.quickanddirtytips.com/education/grammar/understanding-voice-and-tone-in-writing.

[25] Jenny Johnson, 'Can I have your gluten?', Twitter, October 11, 2013, http://twitter.com/JennyJohnsonHi5/status/388517006040784896. See also Jenny Johnson, 'I have so much respect for people who eat inside Taco Bell instead of going through the drive-thru and eating in their car like garbage', Twitter, July 17, 2014, http://twitter.com/JennyJohnsonHi5/status/489518538462199810; Jenny Johnson, 'I'm happy Kim Kardashian is on another vacation in Mexico. She deserves to relax after all the

hard work she's been doing', Twitter, July 19, 2014, http://twitter.com/jennyjohnsonhi5/status/490290476067479552.

[26] Jenny Johnson, Twitter, http://twitter.com/JennyJohnsonHi5.

[27] Taco Bell, Twitter, http://twitter.com/tacobell.

[28] Taco Bell, 'Taco Bell gets me', Twitter, April 11, 2014, http://twitter.com/tacobell/status/454377957692170241. See also Taco Bell, 'Taco Bell is my spirit animal', Twitter, March 8, 2014, http://twitter.com/tacobell/status/442101162875953152; Taco Bell, 'I followed my heart, and it led me to Taco Bell', Twitter, April 18, 2014, http://twitter.com/tacobell/status/456982976887144448.

[29] Sam Kusinitz, '12 Reasons to Integrate Visual Content Into Your Marketing Campaigns [Infographic]', Hubspot Blogs, July 18, 2014, http://blog.hubspot.com/marketing/visual-content-marketing-infographic.

[30] Sam Kusinitz, '12 Reasons to Integrate Visual Content Into Your Marketing Campaigns [Infographic]'.

[31] Ross Durrence, '15 Movies Better Than Books They Were Based On', Dashboard Citizen, February 5, 2014, http://dashboardcitizen.com/movies-better-than-books.

[32] Photos, Facebook Products, http://newsroom.fb.com/products.

[33] Instagram Statistics, Instagram Press, http://instagram.com/press.

[34] YouTube Statistics, YouTube Press, http://www.youtube.com/yt/press/statistics.html.

[35] Aaron Mamiit, 'Gangnam Style by Psy "Breaks" YouTube View Counter: Here's what really happened', TechTimes.com, December 6 (year not specified), http://www.techtimes.com/articles/21555/20141206/gangnam-style-by-psy-breaks-youtube-view-counter-heres-what-really-happened.htm.

[36] Boo, Facebook, http://www.facebook.com/Boo.

[37] About Boo, Facebook, http://www.facebook.com/Boo/info?tab=page_info.

[38] Boo, Facebook, 'i sleep in the nude. wherever i want. whenever i want', May 23, 2014, http://www.facebook.com/Boo/photos/a.100690783253.87226.80329313253/10152489644833254. See also 'small dog, big world', May 15, 2014, http://www.facebook.com/Boo/photos/a.100690783253.87226.80329313253/10152471700858254; 'welcome to monday. how may i help you?', September 25, 2012, http://www.facebook.com/Boo/photos/a.100690783253.87226.80329313253/10151189511393254/?type=1&theater.

[39] Humans of New York, About, http://www.humansofnewyork.com/about.

[40] Humans of New York, Facebook, http://www.facebook.com/humansofnewyork.

[41] Big Fish Presentations, 'A very brief history of storytelling', The Big Fish Blog, February 28, 2012, http://bigfishpresentations.com/2012/02/28/a-very-brief-history-of-storytelling.

[42] Jon Hamm, 'Why Agencies and Brands Need to Embrace True Storytelling: Branded content is not the same thing', *AdWeek*, September 23, 2013, http://www.adweek.com/news/advertising-branding/why-agencies-and-brands-need-embrace-true-storytelling-152534.

[43] See also Rodger Dean Duncan, 'Tap the Power of Storytelling', Forbes.com, January 4, 2014, http://www.forbes.com/sites/rodgerdeanduncan/2014/01/04/tap-the-power-of-storytelling; Tim Nudd, '7 Basic Types of Stories: Which one is your brand telling? Creatives explore humans' archetypal plots', Adweek.com, October 3, 2012, http://www.adweek.com/news/advertising-branding/7-basic-types-stories-which-one-your-brand-telling-144164; The Storytellers, 'The power of storytelling', TheStorytellers.com, http://www.thestorytellers.com/the-power-of-storytelling; and Jon Thomas, '7 Reasons Storytelling Is Important For Branded Content', postadvertising.com, August 15, 2012, http://www.postadvertising.com/2012/08/7-reasons-storytelling-is-important-for-branded-content.

[44] Solis, *WTF [What's the Future] of Business*, p.33.

[45] Facebook Statistics, http://newsroom.fb.com/company-info.

[46] See Arlinda Mezini, 'Corporate Storytelling: Ford makes customers the stars', CEB Blogs, ExecutiveBoard.com, September 2, 2013, http://www.executiveboard.com/blogs/how-ford-makes-customers-the-stars-of-its-corporate-storytelling. See also Neil Patel and Rikita Puri, '*Tell Your Brand's Story*', *The Beginner's Guide to Online Marketing*, Quicksprout.com, Chapter Three, http://www.quicksprout.com/the-beginners-guide-to-online-marketing-chapter-3.

[47] About Coca-Cola, Facebook, http://www.facebook.com/cocacola/info?tab=page_info.

[48] About, Black Milk Clothing, http://blackmilkclothing.com/pages/about-us.

[49] Black Milk Clothing, Instagram, http://instagram.com/blackmilkclothing.

[50] Australia.com, Facebook, http://www.facebook.com/SeeAustralia; see also http://www.facebook.com/SeeAustralia/photos_stream?tab=photos_albums.

[51] Josh Sanburn, 'Does Kmart's Hilarious New Ad Acknowledge That Kmart Stores Are Hopeless?', business.time.com, April 19, 2013, http://business.time.com/2013/04/19/does-kmarts-hilarious-new-ad-acknowledge-that-kmart-stores-are-hopeless. See also Rae Ann Fera, 'How Kmart Used Social Listening (And Some Nerve) To Create A Ship-My-Pants Funny Viral Hit', fastcocreate.com, April, 22 2013, http://www.fastcocreate.com/1682826/how-kmart-used-social-listening-and-some-nerve-to-create-a-ship-my-pants-funny-viral-hit; and Lisa Scherzer, 'Kmart's "Ship My Pants" Ad Gets Laughs. Sales are another story', finance.yahoo.com, April 16, 2013, http://finance.yahoo.com/blogs/the-exchange/kmart-ship-pants-ad-gets-laughs-sales-another-184147601.html.

52 Kmart, 'Ship My Pants' (commercial), YouTube video, 0:35, Kmart, April 10, 2013, http://www.youtube.com/watch?v=I03UmJbK0lA.

53 Laura Heller, '"Ship My Pants": Kmart's unexpected viral hit', Forbes.com, April 15, 2013, http://www.forbes.com/sites/lauraheller/2013/04/15/ship-my-pants-kmarts-unexpected-viral-hit.

54 'Sandwich Shop Advertises Worst Meatball Sandwich of Yelper's Life', The Huffington Post, June 28, 2012, http://www.huffingtonpost.com/2012/06/28/yelp-worst-meatball-sandwich_n_1633755.html.

55 Tim Washer, Content Marketing World Sydney, 2014, permission via e-mail April 6, 2015.

56 Ellen DeGeneres, Goodreads.com, http://www.goodreads.com/quotes/22454-my-grandmother-started-walking-five-miles-a-day-when-she.

57 Lance Pauker, '30 Painfully Funny One-Liners From 30 Legendary Comedians', thoughtcatalogue.com, October 7, 2013, http://thoughtcatalog.com/lance-pauker/2013/10/30-painfully-funny-one-liners-from-30-legendary-comedians.

58 '30 Great One-liners', The Telegraph, (nd), http://www.telegraph.co.uk/culture/culturepicturegalleries/9594011/30-great-one-liners.html.

59 Jerry Seinfeld quotes, Lifehack Quotes, http://quotes.lifehack.org/by-author/jerry-seinfeld.

60 Grumpy Cat, http://www.grumpycats.com.

61 'The 50 Funniest Grumpy Cat Memes', Complex, March 4, 2013, http://www.complex.com/style/2013/03/the-50-funniest-grumpy-cat-memes.

62 Videos, Weird Al Yankovic, http://weirdal.com/videos.

63 Oliver Burkeman, 'Are You Sitting Uncomfortably?', The Guardian, October 11, 2008, http://www.theguardian.com/stage/2008/oct/11/sarah-silverman-comedy.

64 Miley Cyrus, 'Wrecking Ball', YouTube video, 3:41, MileyCyrusVEVO, September 9, 2013, http://www.youtube.com/watch?v=My2FRPA3Gf8.

65 Marc Inocencio, 'Miley Cyrus' "Wrecking Ball" Sets New VEVO Record', RyanSeacrest.com, September 17, 2013, http://www.ryanseacrest.com/2013/09/17/wrecking-ball-music-video-miley-cyrus-5-most-memorable-moments.

66 Casey Brown, 'Mashable Celebrates Digital Culture at SXSWi', Mashable.com, March 13, 2014, http://mashable.com/2014/03/12/mashable-sxswi-recap.

67 Barbie, Facebook, http://www.facebook.com/officialbarbieaustralia.

68 Mattel's Barbie, LinkedIn, http://www.linkedin.com/company/barbie%C2%AE.

69 Oreo, 'You Can Still Dunk in the Dark', Twitter, February 4, 2013, http://twitter.com/oreo/status/298246571718483968.

70 Starbucks, 'And then there were three. Congratulations!', Twitter, July 23, 2013, http://twitter.com/starbucksuk/status/359401066380537857.

71 'The Naked CEO', CPA Australia, http://www.thenakedceo.com.

[72] Gary Vaynerchuck, '#AskGaryVee', http://www.garyvaynerchuk.com/AskGaryVee.

[73] Social Media Examiner, Social Media Marketing podcasts, http://www.socialmediaexaminer.com/tag/social-media-marketing-podcast.

[74] Vincent van Gogh, BrainyQuote.com, http://www.brainyquote.com/quotes/quotes/v/vincentvan104644.html.

[75] 'Nelson Mandela: 11 inspirational quotes to live your life by', *The Independent*, http://www.independent.co.uk/news/world/nelson-mandela-10-inspirational-quotes-to-live-your-life-by-8988290.html?action=gallery.

[76] Rachel Hodin, '35 Famous People Who Were Painfully Rejected Before Making It Big', thoughtcatalogue.com, October 14, 2013, http://thoughtcatalog.com/rachel-hodin/2013/10/35-famous-people-who-were-painfully-rejected-before-making-it-big. See also TrustLeaf, '7 Business Leaders Who Failed Before They Succeeded', Medium.com, November 19, 2013, http://medium.com/@TrustLeaf/7-business-leaders-who-failed-before-they-succeeded-5aad52268873; David Zurawik, 'Oprah – Built in Baltimore', *The Baltimore Sun* (*Sun Magazine*), May 18, 2011, http://articles.baltimoresun.com/2011-05-18/entertainment/bs-sm-oprahs-baltimore-20110522_1_oprah-winfrey-show-baltimore-history-wjz.

[77] Steve Jobs, 'Steve Jobs' 2005 Stanford Commencement Address', YouTube video, 15:04, Stanford, March 7, 2008 (filmed June 12, 2005), http://www.youtube.com/watch?v=UF8uR6Z6KLc. See also 'Steve Jobs' 2005 Stanford Commencement Address', *Stanford News*, June 14, 2005, http://news.stanford.edu/news/2005/june15/videos/987.html.

[78] Thomas Edison, BrainyQuote.com, http://www.brainyquote.com/quotes/quotes/t/thomasaed132683.html.

[79] Richard Branson, BrainyQuote.com, http://www.brainyquote.com/quotes/quotes/r/richardbra452112.html.

[80] Ellen Johnson Sirleaf, Goodreads.com, http://www.goodreads.com/quotes/390551-if-your-dreams-do-not-scare-you-they-are-not.

[81] Facebook Statistics, Facebook Newsroom, http://newsroom.fb.com/company-info.

[82] Interview with Randi Zuckerberg by the author via VOIP, July 8, 2014.

[83] Judy Carter, *The Message of You: Turn your life story into a money-making speaking career*, St. Martin's Press, New York, 2013.

[84] Mark Malkoff, http://markmalkoff.com/about.

[85] Black Milk Clothing, Instagram, http://instagram.com/blackmilkclothing.

[86] Black Milk Clothing, Facebook, http://www.facebook.com/blackmilkclothing.

[87] Brian Solis, http://www.briansolis.com/about.

[88] George Bernard Shaw, BrainyQuote.com, http://www.brainyquote.com/quotes/quotes/g/georgebern109542.html.

89 George Eliot, BrainyQuote.com, http://www.brainyquote.com/quotes/quotes/g/georgeelio161679.htm.

90 Jack London, Goodreads.com, http://www.goodreads.com/quotes/3309-you-can-t-wait-for-inspiration-you-have-to-go-after.

91 Dr John B. Arden, *Rewire Your Brain: Think your way to a better life,* John Wiley & Sons, New Jersey, 2010, p.172.

92 'Sunni Brown: Doodlers, unite!', TED Talk video, 5:50, March 2011, http://www.ted.com/talks/sunni_brown?language=en.

93 Judy Carter, *The Comedy Bible: From stand-up to sitcom – The comedy writer's ultimate 'how to' guide,* Touchstone Books, Simon & Schuster, New York, 2001, p.85.

94 Albert Einstein, Goodreads.com, http://www.goodreads.com/quotes/110518-if-at-first-the-idea-is-not-absurd-then-there.

95 'Potato Salad Kickstarter Ends, Earns Man $55,492', abc7.com, August 04, 2014, http://abc7.com/food/potato-salad-kickstarter-ends-earns-man-$55492/239469. See also Zack Danger Brown, 'Potato Salad: I'm making potato salad', Kickstarter campaign, Kickstarter.com, http://www.kickstarter.com/projects/zackdangerbrown/potato-salad/posts/1292853.

96 Paulo Coelho, Goodreads.com, http://www.goodreads.com/quotes/594264-one-day-you-will-wake-up-there-won-t-be.

REFERENCES

CHAPTER 1

Maya Angelou, Goodreads.com, http://www.goodreads.com/quotes/153929-you-can-t-use-up-creativity-the-more-you-use-the.

Content Marketing Institute, 'What Is Content Marketing?', http://contentmarketinginstitute.com/what-is-content-marketing.

Seth Godin, BrainyQuote.com, http://www.brainyquote.com/quotes/quotes/s/sethgodin541626.html.

Joe Pulizzi, *Epic Content Marketing: How to tell a different story, Break through the clutter, and win more customers by marketing less*, McGraw-Hill Education, Columbus, 2014.

Mark Schaefer, *Social Media Explained: Untangling the world's most misunderstood business trend*, Mark Schaefer, 2014.

Brian Solis, *WTF [What's the Future] of Business: Changing the way businesses create experiences*, John Wiley & Sons, New Jersey, 2013.

Neil Vidyarthi, 'Attention Spans Have Dropped from 12 Minutes to 5 Minutes — How social media is ruining our minds [Infographic]', AdWeek/SocialTimes, December 14, 2011, http://www.adweek.com/socialtimes/attention-spans-have-dropped-from-12-minutes-to-5-seconds-how-social-media-is-ruining-our-minds-infographic.

CHAPTER 2

Jeff Goins, '5 Easy Tricks to Help You Write Catchy Headlines', goinswriter.com, (nd), http://goinswriter.com/catchy-headlines.

Megan Marrs, '19 Headline Writing Tips for More Clickable, Shareable Blog Posts', WordStream, July 17, 2014, http://www.wordstream.com/blog/ws/2014/07/17/headline-writing.

CHAPTER 3

Thomas Armitage, '101 Different Types of Content', *Ragan's PR Daily*, May 7, 2014, http://www.prdaily.com/Main/Articles/101_different_types_of_content_16375.aspx.

George Beahm, ed, *I, Steve: Steve Jobs in his own words*, Hardie Grant Books, Melbourne, Kindle edition, 2011. Quote from the Apple Worldwide Developers Conference, San Jose Convention Center, California, May 13–16, 1997.

Allyson Galle, '14 Unique Types of Content Every Marketer Should Try', Hubspot Blogs, June 21, 2012, http://blog.hubspot.com/blog/tabid/6307/bid/33284/14-Unique-Types-of-Content-Every-Marketer-Should-Try.aspx.

Brandon Griggs, '10 Great Quotes from Steve Jobs', CNN, October 9, 2012, http://edition.cnn.com/2012/10/04/tech/innovation/steve-jobs-quotes. Quote from Apple Worldwide Developers Conference, 1997.

CHAPTER 4

Lisa Baertlein, 'Ellen's Oscar "selfie" crashes Twitter, breaks record', Reuters.com, March 3, 2014, http://www.reuters.com/article/2014/03/03/us-oscars-selfie-idUSBREA220C320140303.

Sandra Blakeslee, 'Complex and Hidden Brain in Gut Makes Stomachaches and Butterflies', New York Times, January 23, 1996, http://www.nytimes.com/1996/01/23/science/complex-and-hidden-brain-in-gut-makes-stomachaches-and-butterflies.html.

Ellen DeGeneres selfie, 'If only Bradley's arm was longer. Best photo ever. #oscars', Twitter, March 3, 2014, http://twitter.com/theellenshow/status/440322224407314432.

Dove United States, 'Dove Real Beauty Sketches | You're more beautiful than you think', YouTube video, 3:00, doveunitedstates, April 14, 2013, http://www.youtube.com/watch?v=XpaOjMXyJGk.

Emma Gray, 'Dove's "Real Beauty Sketches" Ad Campaign Tells Women "You're More Beautiful Than You Think"', The Huffington Post, April 17, 2013, http://www.huffingtonpost.com/2013/04/15/doves-real-beauty-sketches-ad-campaign-video_n_3088071.html.

Jason Keath, 'The Top 11 Branded Viral Videos of 2013', socialfresh.com, January 8, 2014, http://www.socialfresh.com/top-branded-viral-videos-2013.

Laura Stampler, 'How Dove's "Real Beauty Sketches" Became the Most Viral Video Ad of All Time', BusinessInsider.com.au, May 23, 2013, http://www.businessinsider.com.au/how-doves-real-beauty-sketches-became-the-most-viral-ad-video-of-all-time-2013-5.

CHAPTER 5

Jonah Berger, 'Viral's Secret Formula', The Huffington Post, June 10, 2013, http://www.huffingtonpost.com/jonah-berger/virals-secret-formula_b_3052685.html.

Jack Shepherd, 'How to Make Something Go Viral: Tips from BuzzFeed', The Guardian, March 17, 2014, http://www.theguardian.com/media/2014/mar/16/how-to-make-something-go-viral-tips-buzzfeed.

Alyson Shontell, 'INSIDE BUZZFEED: The story of how Jonah Peretti built the web's most beloved new media brand', Business Insider Australia, December 12, 2012, http://www.businessinsider.com.au/buzzfeed-jonah-peretti-interview-2012-12.

CHAPTER 6

Ellen DeGeneres, 'Ellen at Tulane Commencement 2009', YouTube video, 17:54, Tulane University, March 4, 2010, http://www.youtube.com/watch?v=0e8ToRVOtRo; see also Forbes, 'The World's Highest-Paid Celebrities, 2015 ranking: #12 Ellen DeGeneres', Forbes.com, http://www.forbes.com/profile/ellen-degeneres.

Walt Disney, BrainyQuote.com, http://www.brainyquote.com/quotes/quotes/w/waltdisney130027.html.

Steve Jobs, Quotationspage.com, http://www.quotationspage.com/quote/38353.html.

Steve Jobs, 'Steve Jobs' 2005 Stanford Commencement Address', YouTube video, 15:04, Stanford, March 7, 2008 (filmed June 12, 2005), http://www.youtube.com/watch?v=UF8uR6Z6KLc. See also 'Steve Jobs' 2005 Stanford Commencement Address', *Stanford News*, June 14, 2005, http://news.stanford.edu/news/2005/june15/videos/987.html.

Michael Jordan, BrainyQuote.com, http://www.brainyquote.com/quotes/quotes/m/michaeljor167382.html.

Lady Gaga: see Lady Gaga's 'Born This Way', YouTube video, 7:19, LadyGaga VEVO, February 27, 2011, http://www.youtube.com/watch?v=wV1FrqwZyKw; see also Lady Gaga, Goodreads.com, http://www.goodreads.com/author/quotes/2945649.Lady_Gaga.

Malinda Lo, 'Back in the Day: Coming out with Ellen', AfterEllen.com, April 9, 2005, http://www.afterellen.com/tv/34682-back-in-the-day-coming-out-with-ellen.

J.K. Rowling, BrainyQuote.com, http://www.brainyquote.com/quotes/quotes/j/jkrowlin415661.html.

Steven Spielberg, BrainyQuote.com, http://www.brainyquote.com/quotes/quotes/s/stevenspie113970.html.

Mae West, Goodreads.com, http://www.goodreads.com/quotes/1598-you-only-live-once-but-if-you-do-it-right.

Oscar Wilde, Goodreads.com, http://www.goodreads.com/quotes/19884-be-yourself-everyone-else-is-already-taken.

CHAPTER 7

Mike Ayers, 'Psy's "Gangnam Style" Is Most-Watched Video on YouTube', *The Wall Street Journal*, December 4, 2014, www.wsj.com/articles/gangnam-re-styles-youtube-1417660563.

Justin Bieber, YouTube videos, http://www.youtube.com/user/kidrauhl/videos.

Boo the Pomeranian, 'Boo, The World's Cutest Dog, Takes Over Times Square on Jumbotron', YouTube video, 3:41, ABC News, September 9, 2011, http://www.youtube.com/watch?v=Y3mIPM-7rKM; see also Boo the Dog, http://www.boothedog.net; Boo, Facebook, http://www.facebook.com/Boo; About Boo, Facebook, http://www.facebook.

com/Boo/info?tab=page_info; 'i sleep in the nude. wherever i want. whenever i want.', May 23, 2014, http://www.facebook.com/Boo/phot os/a.100690783253.87226.80329313253/10152489644833254; 'just a couple of dudes with pretty great hair hanging out. no big deal. Liam Payne One Direction', November 25, 2014, http://www.facebook.com/Boo/pho tos/a.100690783253.87226.80329313253/10152952876173254; 'small dog, big world.', May 15, 2014, http://www.facebook.com/Boo/photos /a.100690783253.87226.80329313253/10152471700858254; 'welcome to monday. how may i help you?', September 25, 2012, http://www.facebook. com/Boo/photos/a.100690783253.87226.80329313253/10151189511 393254/?type=1&theater; Boo, Wikipedia, http://en.wikipedia.org/wiki/ Boo_%28dog%29.

Erica Cerulo, '4 Ways to Nail Your Brand Voice', Mashable.com, June 27, 2014, http://mashable.com/2014/06/26/brand-voice-tips.

Harriet Cummings, 'Content Marketers: Concrete Steps To Finding Your Brand's Voice', Marketing Land, February 26, 2014, http://marketingland. com/shape-tone-voice-74297.

Ross Durrence, '15 Movies Better Than Books They Were Based On', Dashboard Citizen, February 5, 2014, http://dashboardcitizen.com/ movies-better-than-books.

Facebook Photos, Facebook Products, http://newsroom.fb.com/products.

Larissa Faw, 'Millennial YouTube Star Michelle Phan's Keys To Success', Forbes. com, June 5, 2014, http://www.forbes.com/sites/larissafaw/2014/06/05/ millennial-youtube-star-michelle-phans-keys-to-success.

Cris Freese, 'Voice in Writing: Developing a unique writing voice', Writer's Digest, September 12, 2013, http://www.writersdigest.com/editor-blogs/ there-are-no-rules/voice-in-writing-developing-a-unique-writing-voice.

Jeff Goins, '10 Steps to Finding Your Writing Voice', Goins, Writer, (nd), http://goinswriter.com/writing-voice.

Humans of New York, http://www.humansofnewyork.com; see also http://www.humansofnewyork.com/about; http://www.facebook.com/ humansofnewyork.

Instagram Statistics, Instagram Press, http://instagram.com/press.

Jenny Johnson, 'Can I have your gluten?', Twitter, October 11, 2013, http:// twitter.com/JennyJohnsonHi5/status/388517006040784896; 'I have so much respect for people who eat inside Taco Bell instead of going through the drive-thru and eating in their car like garbage', Twitter, July 17, 2014, http://twitter.com/JennyJohnsonHi5/status/489518538462199810; 'I'm happy Kim Kardashian is on another vacation in Mexico. She deserves to relax after all the hard work she's been doing', Twitter, July 19, 2014, http://twitter.com/jennyjohnsonhi5/status/490290476067479552.

Joel Klettke, 'Finding Your Brand Voice (Without Losing Your Mind)', iAcquire.com, January 6, 2014, http://www.iacquire.com/blog/finding-your-brand-voice-without-losing-your-mind.

Sam Kusinitz, '12 Reasons to Integrate Visual Content Into Your Marketing Campaigns [Infographic]', Hubspot Blogs, July 18, 2014, http://blog.hubspot.com/marketing/visual-content-marketing-infographic.

Aaron Mamiit, 'Gangnam Style by Psy "Breaks" YouTube View Counter: Here's what really happened', TechTimes.com, December 6 (year not specified), http://www.techtimes.com/articles/21555/20141206/gangnam-style-by-psy-breaks-youtube-view-counter-heres-what-really-happened.htm.

Psy, 'Gangnam Style', YouTube video, 4:12, officialpsy, July 15, 2012, http://www.youtube.com/watch?v=9bZkp7q19f0.

Taco Bell, Twitter, http://twitter.com/tacobell; see also 'Taco Bell gets me', Twitter, April 11, 2014, http://twitter.com/tacobell/status/454377957692170241; 'Taco Bell is my spirit animal', Twitter, March 8, 2014, http://twitter.com/tacobell/status/442101162875953152; 'I followed my heart, and it led me to Taco Bell', Twitter, April 18, 2014, http://twitter.com/tacobell/status/456982976887144448.

Ekaterina Walter, 'The Rise Of Visual Social Media', fastcompany.com, August 28, 2012, http://www.fastcompany.com/3000794/rise-visual-social-media.

Julie Wildhaber, 'Understanding Voice and Tone in Writing: Choosing words to connect with your audience', Grammar Girl – quickanddirtytips.com, July 1, 2010, http://www.quickanddirtytips.com/education/grammar/understanding-voice-and-tone-in-writing.

YouTube Statistics, YouTube Press, http://www.youtube.com/yt/press/statistics.html.

CHAPTER 8

Australia.com, Facebook, http://www.facebook.com/SeeAustralia. See also http://www.facebook.com/SeeAustralia/photos_stream?tab=photos_albums.

Leah Betancourt, '10 Rules for Increasing Community Engagement', Mashable.com, December 16, 2009, http://mashable.com/2009/12/16/community-engagement.

Big Fish Presentations, 'A very brief history of storytelling', The Big Fish Blog, February 28, 2012, http://bigfishpresentations.com/2012/02/28/a-very-brief-history-of-storytelling.

Black Milk Clothing, http://blackmilkclothing.com; see also http://blackmilkclothing.com/pages/about-us; Black Milk Clothing, Facebook, http://www.facebook.com/blackmilkclothing; Black Milk Clothing, Instagram, http://instagram.com/blackmilkclothing; Black Milk Clothing customer order letter.

CNN, 'Mark Zuckerberg Fast Facts', CNN, May 22, 2015, http://edition.cnn.com/2013/05/07/us/mark-zuckerberg-fast-facts.

About Coca-Cola, Facebook, http://www.facebook.com/cocacola/info?tab=page_info.

Rodger Dean Duncan, 'Tap the Power of Storytelling', Forbes.com, January 4, 2014, http://www.forbes.com/sites/rodgerdeanduncan/2014/01/04/tap-the-power-of-storytelling.

Facebook Statistics, http://newsroom.fb.com/company-info.

Rae Ann Fera, 'How Kmart Used Social Listening (and Some Nerve) to Create a Ship-My-Pants Funny Viral Hit', fastcocreate.com, April 22, 2013, http://www.fastcocreate.com/1682826/how-kmart-used-social-listening-and-some-nerve-to-create-a-ship-my-pants-funny-viral-hit.

Jon Hamm, 'Why Agencies and Brands Need to Embrace True Storytelling: Branded content is not the same thing', Adweek, September 23, 2013, http://www.adweek.com/news/advertising-branding/why-agencies-and-brands-need-embrace-true-storytelling-152534.

Laura Heller, '"Ship My Pants": Kmart's unexpected viral hit', Forbes.com. http://www.forbes.com/sites/lauraheller/2013/04/15/ship-my-pants-kmarts-unexpected-viral-hit.

'Sandwich Shop Advertises Worst Meatball Sandwich of Yelper's Life', The Huffington Post, June 28, 2012, http://www.huffingtonpost.com/2012/06/28/yelp-worst-meatball-sandwich_n_1633755.html.

Joe and Misses Doe, http://joeandmissesdoe.com.

Kmart, 'Ship My Pants' (commercial), YouTube video, 0:35, Kmart, April 10, 2013, http://www.youtube.com/watch?v=I03UmJbK0lA.

Arlinda Mezini, 'Corporate Storytelling: Ford makes customers the stars', CEB Blogs, ExecutiveBoard.com, September 2, 2013, http://www.executiveboard.com/blogs/how-ford-makes-customers-the-stars-of-its-corporate-storytelling.

Tim Nudd, '7 Basic Types of Stories: Which one is your brand telling? Creatives explore humans' archetypal plots', Adweek, October 3, 2012, http://www.adweek.com/news/advertising-branding/7-basic-types-stories-which-one-your-brand-telling-144164.

Neil Patel and Rikita Puri, 'Tell Your Brand's Story', The Beginner's Guide to Online Marketing, Quicksprout.com, Chapter Three, http://www.quicksprout.com/the-beginners-guide-to-online-marketing-chapter-3.

Josh Sanburn, 'Does Kmart's Hilarious New Ad Acknowledge That Kmart Stores Are Hopeless?', business.time.com, April 19, 2013, http://business.time.com/2013/04/19/does-kmarts-hilarious-new-ad-acknowledge-that-kmart-stores-are-hopeless.

Lisa Scherzer, 'Kmart's "Ship My Pants" Ad Gets Laughs. Sales are another story', finance.yahoo.com, April 16, 2013, http://finance.yahoo.

com/blogs/the-exchange/kmart-ship-pants-ad-gets-laughs-sales-another-184147601.html.

Brian Solis, *WTF [What's the Future] of Business: Changing the way businesses create experiences*, John Wiley & Sons, New Jersey, 2013.

The Storytellers, 'The power of storytelling', TheStorytellers.com, http://www.thestorytellers.com/the-power-of-storytelling.

Jon Thomas, '7 Reasons Storytelling Is Important For Branded Content', postadvertising.com, August 15, 2012, http://www.postadvertising.com/2012/08/7-reasons-storytelling-is-important-for-branded-content.

Tourism Australia, 'The World's Biggest Social Media Team', February 15, 2013, http://www.slideshare.net/TourismAustralia/the-worlds-biggest-social-media-team-16545786.

CHAPTER 9

Oliver Burkeman, 'Are you sitting uncomfortably?', *The Guardian*, October 11, 2008, http://www.theguardian.com/stage/2008/oct/11/sarah-silverman-comedy.

Judy Carter, *The Comedy Bible: From stand-up to sitcom – The comedy writer's ultimate 'how to' guide*, Touchstone Books, Simon & Schuster, New York, 2001.

'The 50 Funniest Grumpy Cat Memes', Complex, March 4, 2013, http://www.complex.com/style/2013/03/the-50-funniest-grumpy-cat-memes.

Christian Cook, 'What is Comedy and What Makes Something Funny?', (nd), http://www.thinctanc.co.uk/words/comedy.html.

Greg Dean, *Step by Step to Stand-up Comedy*, Heinemann, New Hampshire, 2000.

Ellen DeGeneres, Goodreads.com, http://www.goodreads.com/quotes/22454-my-grandmother-started-walking-five-miles-a-day-when-she.

Grumpy Cat, http://www.grumpycats.com.

Jason Lipshutz, 'Weird Al' Yankovic's 10 Funniest Songs: "Eat It," "Pretty Fly for a Rabbi" & More', Billboard.com, July 16, 2014, http://www.billboard.com/articles/columns/pop-shop/6157853/weird-al-yankovic-10-funniest-songs-ever.

Jan McInnis, *Finding the Funny Fast: How to create quick humor to connect with clients, coworkers and crowds*, Cubicle Comedy, 2009.

Lance Pauker, '30 Painfully Funny One-Liners From 30 Legendary Comedians', thoughtcatalogue.com, October 7, 2013, http://thoughtcatalog.com/lance-pauker/2013/10/30-painfully-funny-one-liners-from-30-legendary-comedians.

Jerry Seinfeld quotes, Lifehack Quotes, http://quotes.lifehack.org/by-author/jerry-seinfeld.

'30 Great One-liners', *The Telegraph*, (nd) http://www.telegraph.co.uk/culture/culturepicturegalleries/9594011/30-great-one-liners.html.

John Vorhaus, *The Comic Toolbox: How to be funny even if you're not*, Silman-James Press, Los Angeles, 1994.

Weird Al Yankovic videos, http://weirdal.com/videos.

CHAPTER 10

Barbie, Mattel, Facebook, http://www.facebook.com/officialbarbieaustralia; see also 'Barbie Entrepreneur Doll', Mattel shop, Barbie.com, http://www.barbie.com/en-us/shop/productdetail?id=34844196&productxxx=1&ProductName=BARBIE-Entrepreneur-Doll; see also Barbie LinkedIn, http://www.linkedin.com/company/barbie%C2%AE.

Casey Brown, 'Mashable Celebrates Digital Culture at SXSWi', Mashable.com, March 13, 2014, http://mashable.com/2014/03/12/mashable-sxswi-recap.

Casey Brown, 'Snap a Selfie on a Wrecking Ball at the Mashable House SXSWi', Mashable.com, February 26, 2014, http://mashable.com/2014/02/25/sxsw-mashable-house-wrecking-ball.

Brian Clark, '22 Ways to Create Compelling Content When You Don't Have a Clue [Infographic]', Copyblogger, (nd), http://www.copyblogger.com/create-content-infographic.

Miley Cyrus, 'Wrecking Ball', YouTube video, 3:41, MileyCyrusVEVO, September 9, 2013, http://www.youtube.com/watch?v=My2FRPA3Gf8.

Marc Inocencio, 'Miley Cyrus' "Wrecking Ball" Sets New VEVO Record', RyanSeacrest.com, September 17, 2013, http://www.ryanseacrest.com/2013/09/17/wrecking-ball-music-video-miley-cyrus-5-most-memorable-moments.

Oreo, 'You can still dunk in the dark', Twitter, February 4, 2013, http://twitter.com/oreo/status/298246571718483968.

Starbucks, 'And then there were three. Congratulations!', Twitter, July 23, 2013, http://twitter.com/starbucksuk/status/359401066380537857.

'Top 100 Movie Quotes', Information Please, (nd), http://www.infoplease.com/ipea/A0931686.html.

Pat Yasinskas, '"Abnormality" caused power outage', ESPN, February 5, 2013, http://espn.go.com/nfl/playoffs/2012/story/_/id/8911864/2013-super-bowl-power-outage-stops-game-super-bowl-xlvii.

CHAPTER 11

Canva, http://www.canva.com.

Brian Clark, '22 Ways to Create Compelling Content When You Don't Have a Clue [Infographic]', Copyblogger, (nd), http://www.copyblogger.com/create-content-infographic.

Instaquote (app), http://itunes.apple.com/au/app/instaquote-add-text-captions/id551012097?mt=8.

The Naked CEO, CPA Australia, http://www.thenakedceo.com.

Over, http://madewithover.com.

Social Media Examiner, 'Your Guide to the Social Media Jungle', Social Media Examiner, http://www.socialmediaexaminer.com; see also http://www.socialmediaexaminer.com/tag/social-media-marketing-podcast.

Gary Vaynerchuck, '#AskGaryVee', http://www.garyvaynerchuk.com/AskGaryVee.

CHAPTER 12

Richard Branson, BrainyQuote.com, http://www.brainyquote.com/quotes/quotes/r/richardbra452112.html.

Thomas Edison, BrainyQuote.com, http://www.brainyquote.com/quotes/quotes/t/thomasaed132683.html.

Facebook Statistics, http://newsroom.fb.com/company-info.

Rachel Hodin, '35 Famous People Who Were Painfully Rejected Before Making It Big', thoughtcatalogue.com, October 14, 2013, http://thoughtcatalog.com/rachel-hodin/2013/10/35-famous-people-who-were-painfully-rejected-before-making-it-big.

Steve Jobs, 'Steve Jobs' 2005 Stanford Commencement Address', YouTube video, 15:04, Stanford, March 7, 2008 (filmed June 12, 2005), http://www.youtube.com/watch?v=UF8uR6Z6KLc; see also 'Steve Jobs' 2005 Stanford Commencement Address', Stanford News, June 14, 2005, http://news.stanford.edu/news/2005/june15/videos/987.html.

'Nelson Mandela: 11 inspirational quotes to live your life by', The Independent, http://www.independent.co.uk/news/world/nelson-mandela-10-inspirational-quotes-to-live-your-life-by-8988290.html?action=gallery.

Ellen Johnson Sirleaf, Goodreads.com, http://www.goodreads.com/quotes/390551-if-your-dreams-do-not-scare-you-they-are-not.

TrustLeaf, '7 Business Leaders Who Failed Before They Succeeded', Medium.com, November 19, 2013, http://medium.com/@TrustLeaf/7-business-leaders-who-failed-before-they-succeeded-5aad52268873.

Vincent van Gogh, BrainyQuote.com, http://www.brainyquote.com/quotes/quotes/v/vincentvan104644.html.

Ekaterina Walter, 'Fail Your Way To Amazing Things', Forbes.com, October 29, 2013, http://www.forbes.com/sites/ekaterinawalter/2013/10/29/fail-your-way-to-amazing-things.

Guy Winch PhD, '10 Signs That You Might Have Fear of Failure ... and 2 ways to overcome it and succeed', PsychologyToday.com (The Squeaky Wheel), June 18, 2013, http://www.psychologytoday.com/blog/the-squeaky-wheel/201306/10-signs-you-might-have-fear-failure.

David Zurawik, 'Oprah – Built in Baltimore', The Baltimore Sun (Sun Magazine), May 18, 2011, http://articles.baltimoresun.com/2011-05-18/entertainment/bs-sm-oprahs-baltimore-20110522_1_oprah-winfrey-show-baltimore-history-wjz.

CHAPTER 13

Altimeter Group, http://www.altimetergroup.com.

Behind the Brand, 'Brian Solis – The end of business as usual from', YouTube video, 34:47, Behind the Brand, April 18, 2010, http://www.youtube.com/watch?v=cU2yzDZRMwk.

Black Milk, http://blackmilkclothing.com; see also Black Milk, Facebook, http://www.facebook.com/blackmilkclothing; Black Milk, Instagram, http://instagram.com/blackmilkclothing.

Judy Carter, *The Message of You: Turn your life story into a money-making speaking career*, St. Martin's Press, New York, 2013.

Judy Carter, http://judycarter.com; see also 'Judy Carter', Wikipedia, http://en.wikipedia.org/wiki/Judy_Carter.

Content Marketing Institute, http://contentmarketinginstitute.com.

Bryan Elliot, 'Why No Brand Is Too Big to Fail, Too Small to Succeed', Bryan Elliott interviews Brian Solis, Mashable.com, April 27, 2012, http://mashable.com/2012/04/27/brian-solis-behind-the-brand.

Mark Malkoff, http://markmalkoff.com; see also '171 Starbucks', YouTube video, 10:54, Mark Malkoff, July 16, 2007, http://www.youtube.com/watch?v=CwYxuV2dVzw; 'Apple Store Challenge', YouTube video, 3:35, My Damn Channel, July 25, 2011, http://www.youtube.com/watch?v=Bo2p82aTQzo; 'Big Wheel vs. Bus – Mark Malkoff', YouTube video, 3:15, My Damn Channel, April 6, 2011, http://www.youtube.com/watch?v=uv916r2UcaU; 'Celebrity Sleepovers', YouTube video, 5:50, markmalkoff/My Damn Channel video, January 24, 2012, http://www.youtube.com/watch?v=19Zf0at1b3Q; 'Mark Malkoff Gets Carried in New York City', YouTube video, 10:18, Mark Malkoff, January 28, 2010, http://www.youtube.com/watch?v=Gi4ClspNrNs; 'Mark Moves Into IKEA', YouTube video, 3:57, Mark Malkoff, January 8, 2008, http://www.youtube.com/watch?v=z3S5s3EITcQ.

Pivot Conference, http://pivotcon.com.

Joe Pulizzi, http://joepulizzi.com; see also 'Junta42 Launches Content Marketing Institute', Z Squared Media, June 16, 2010, http://zsquaredmedia.com/junta42-launches-content-marketing-institute.

Brian Solis, http://www.briansolis.com.

Brian Solis, *WTF [What's the Future] of Business: Changing the way businesses create experiences*, John Wiley & Sons, New Jersey, 2013.

United Nations Foundation, 'Who We Are: Randi Zuckerberg', http://www.unfoundation.org/who-we-are/experts/global-entrepreneurs-council/2011/randi-zuckerberg.html.

Randi Zuckerberg, *Dot Complicated: Untangling our wired lives*, HarperOne/HarperCollins, New York, 2013.

Zuckerberg Media, http://zuckerbergmedia.com.

CHAPTER 14

Dr John B. Arden, *Rewire Your Brain: Think your way to a better life*, John Wiley & Sons, New Jersey, 2010.

Sunni Brown, 'Doodlers, unite!', TED Talk video, 5:50, March 2011, http://www.ted.com/talks/sunni_brown?language=en.

Albert Einstein, Goodreads.com, http://www.goodreads.com/quotes/110518-if-at-first-the-idea-is-not-absurd-then-there.

George Eliot, BrainyQuote.com, http://www.brainyquote.com/quotes/quotes/g/georgeelio161679.htm.

Anna Farmery, '10 Ideas For Creating Compelling Content', The Engaging Brand, March 6, 2014, http://www.theengagingbrand.com/2014/03/10-ideas-for-creating-compelling-content.html.

Larry Kim, '9 Ways to Become More Creative in the Next 10 Minutes', Inc.com, August 11, 2014, http://www.inc.com/larry-kim/9-ways-to-become-more-creative-in-the-next-10-minutes.html.

Jack London, Goodreads.com, http://www.goodreads.com/quotes/3309-you-can-t-wait-for-inspiration-you-have-to-go-after.

George Bernard Shaw, BrainyQuote.com, http://www.brainyquote.com/quotes/quotes/g/georgebern109542.html.

GLOSSARY

Kipp Bodnar, 'The Ultimate Glossary: 120 social media marketing terms explained', HubSpot Blogs, December 30, 2011, http://blog.hubspot.com/blog/tabid/6307/bid/6126/The-Ultimate-Glossary-120-Social-Media-Marketing-Terms-Explained.aspx.

Sean Fagan, 'Which Disney Princess Are You?', BuzzFeed.com, February 4, 2014, www.buzzfeed.com/mccarricksean/which-disney-princes-are-you.

Keely Flaherty, 'Which "Buffy The Vampire Slayer" Character Are You?', BuzzFeed.com, March 21, 2014, http://www.buzzfeed.com/keelyflaherty/which-buffy-the-vampire-slayer-character-are-you.

Matt Foulger, 'The 2014 Social Media Glossary: 154 essential definitions', Hootsuite Blog, http://blog.hootsuite.com/social-media-managers-definitive-glossary-2014.

'Potato salad Kickstarter ends, earns man $55,492', abc7.com, August 04, 2014, http://abc7.com/food/potato-salad-kickstarter-ends-earnsman-$55492/239469. See also Zack Danger Brown, 'Potato Salad: I'm making potato salad', Kickstarter campaign, Kickstarter.com, http://www.kickstarter.com/projects/zackdangerbrown/potato-salad/posts/1292853.

THANK YOU

Paulo Coelho, Goodreads.com, http://www.goodreads.com/quotes/594264-one-day-you-will-wake-up-there-won-t-be.

Recommended Reading/ Listening/Watching

BOOKS

Be a Great Stand-Up by Logan Murray

[The] Bedwetter: Stories of courage, redemption, and pee by Sarah Silverman

Born Standing Up: A comic's life by Steve Martin

[The] Cheeky Monkey: Writing narrative comedy by Tim Ferguson

[The] Comic Toolbox: How to be funny even if you're not by John Vorhaus

Contagious: Why things catch on by Jonah Berger

Content Inc: How entrepreneurs use content to build massive audiences and create radically successful businesses by Joe Pulizzi

Dot Complicated: Untangling our wired lives by Randi Zuckerberg

[The] Emotion Thesaurus: A writer's guide to character expression by Angela Ackerman and Becca Puglisi

Epic Content Marketing: How to tell a different story, Break through the clutter, and win more customers by marketing less by Joe Pulizzi

Everybody Writes: Your go-to guide to creating ridiculously good content by Ann Handley

Finding the Funny Fast: How to create quick humor to connect with clients, coworkers and crowds by Jan McInnis

How to Write Selling Humor (audiobook) by Peter Mehlman and Mel Helitzer

Jab, Jab, Jab, Right Hook: How to tell your story in a noisy social world by Gary Vaynerchuk

[The] Message of You: Turn your life story into a money-making speaking career by Judy Carter

[The] Power of Visual Storytelling: How to use visuals, videos, and social media to market your brand by Ekaterina Walter and Jessica Gioglio

Return On Influence: The revolutionary power of klout, social scoring, and influence marketing by Mark W. Schaefer

Rewire Your Brain: Think your way to a better life by Dr John B. Arden

Seinlanguage by Jerry Seinfeld

Seriously … I'm kidding by Ellen DeGeneres

Step by Step to Stand-Up Comedy by Greg Dean

Think Like Zuck: The five business secrets of Facebook's improbably brilliant CEO Mark Zuckerberg by Ekaterina Walter

WTF [What's the Future] of Business: Changing the way businesses create experiences by Brian Solis

WEBSITES AND BLOGS

Buffer, http://blog.bufferapp.com
Jeff Bullas, http://www.jeffbullas.com
Judy Carter, http://blog.judycarter.com
Content Marketing Institute, http://contentmarketinginstitute.com/blog
Contently, http://contently.com/strategist
Convince and Convert, http://www.convinceandconvert.com/blog
Copyblogger, http://www.copyblogger.com/blog
Digital Trends, http://www.digitaltrends.com
Entrepreneur, http://www.entrepreneur.com
Seth Godin, http://sethgodin.typepad.com
Jeff Goins, http://goinswriter.com
Grumpy Cat, http://www.grumpycats.com
HubSpot, http://blog.hubspot.com
Humans of New York, http://www.humansofnewyork.com
Inc., http://www.inc.com
MarketingProfs, http://www.marketingprofs.com/marketing/library
Mashable, http://mashable.com
Quick Sprout, http://www.quicksprout.com/blog
Social Media Examiner, http://www.socialmediaexaminer.com
Brian Solis, http://www.briansolis.com
Splashbox (online marketing), http://www.splashbox.com.au
Sprout Social, http://sproutsocial.com/insights
Unruly (video marketing research), http://unruly.co/insight/#whitepapers

PODCASTS & VIDEOS

'171 Starbucks' by Mark Malkoff, http://www.youtube.com/watch?v=CwYxuV2dVzw.

'[The] Accidental Creative' by Todd Henry, http://www.accidentalcreative.com/category/podcasts.

'Apple Store Challenge' by Mark Malkoff, 2011, http://www.youtube.com/watch?v=Bo2p82aTQzo.

'#AskGaryVee' by Gary Vaynerchuk, http://www.garyvaynerchuk.com/AskGaryVee.

'Born This Way' by Lady Gaga, http://www.youtube.com/watch?v=wV1FrqwZyKw.

'Celebrity Sleepovers' by Mark Malkoff, http://www.youtube.com/

watch?v=19Zf0at1b3Q.

'Content Inc' by Joe Pulizzi, http://contentmarketinginstitute.com/content-inc-podcast.

'[The] Creative Penn' by Joanna Penn, http://www.thecreativepenn.com/podcasts.

'Doodlers, unite!', TED Talk by Sunni Brown, http://www.ted.com/talks/sunni_brown.

'Entrepreneur on Fire' by John Lee Dumas, http://www.entrepreneuronfire.com/podcast.

'How to build your creative confidence', TED Talk by David Kelley, http://www.ted.com/talks/david_kelley_how_to_build_your_creative_confidence.

'Mark Moves Into IKEA' by Mark Malkoff, http://www.youtube.com/watch?v=z3S5s3EITcQ.

'PNR: This Old Marketing' by Joe Pulizzi and Robert Rose, http://contentmarketinginstitute.com/pnr-with-this-old-marketing-podcast.

'Smart Passive Income' by Pat Flynn, http://www.smartpassiveincome.com/category/podcast.

'Social Media Marketing' by Mike Stelzner, http://www.socialmediaexaminer.com/podcasts.

'Steve Jobs' 2005 Stanford Commencement Address', Steve Jobs at Stanford University, http://news.stanford.edu/news/2005/june15/videos/987.html.

Steven Spielberg's Academy of Achievement speech, http://www.youtube.com/watch?v=I5_cGrNoRd0.

'The Pivot, Marketing Backstories' by Todd Wheatland, Content Marketing Institute, http://contentmarketinginstitute.com/the-pivot-marketing-backstories.

'Unmarketing' by Scott Stratten and Alison Kramer, http://www.unmarketing.com/category/podcast.

'Your elusive creative genius', TED Talk by Elizabeth Gilbert http://www.ted.com/talks/elizabeth_gilbert_on_genius.